I Was Born This Way

Allison Wetherbee

authorHOUSE®

AuthorHouse™
1663 Liberty Drive, Suite 200
Bloomington, IN 47403
www.authorhouse.com
Phone: 1-800-839-8640

First published by AuthorHouse 12/15/2008

ISBN: 978-1-4389-3594-2 (sc)

Printed in the United States of America
Bloomington, Indiana

This book is printed on acid-free paper.

Note:
All scripture is taken from the New Living Translation using BibleGateway.com.
For more information about Easter Seals Camp ASCCA, please visit: www.campascca.org

Front cover photograph taken by Geni L. Payne
with illustrations by Allison Wetherbee

Contents

Photographs

Part Two: Devotions and Inspirations

Thank You

IF I MADE A LIST of my blessings, it would stretch around the world one hundred times and still not be complete. God has given me all I need and then some. Throughout the years, He has provided exactly the right people at exactly the right times to push me into my destiny. There is no "thank you" that could ever convey the tremendous gratitude I feel for everyone who has loved and helped me throughout my life.

As a professional counselor, one of my regular exercises is to ask my clients to name their "celebrations." Celebrations include blessings, good news, and the people to whom my clients are thankful. I would like to take this opportunity for my own celebration! I celebrate my parents, Charlie and Gloria Wetherbee, my sisters, Dana and Megan, as well as my extended family. I celebrate my friends and every single person who encouraged the writing of this book with special thanks to authors, Trey Wickwire and Avin Benn, for helping me begin and finish this project. I celebrate you all, and I thank you from the bottom of my heart.

At the present time, I continue to live independently with the help of live-in attendants. My mother visits me once a month to give my attendants time off. I work full-time as a mental health therapist, and

I enjoy my home, my family, and my friends. I am truly blessed, and I reverently thank God. He has shown me that my fears are resolved in His time. He has made old dreams come true, leaving room for new ones. He creates ways to remind me of my worth whenever I question it.

He has even found a way to use every mistake I've made to place me on a road that has led to pure goodness. He has led me to discover for myself who I truly am. Once we each discover that knowledge, our only limits are those we create.

Allison Wetherbee
August 2007

Preface

I WAS HAPPY IN THE weeks before Christmas of 2005. I had defied the odds and done what most people, including myself, had once thought impossible; I had accomplished independence. I no longer had anything to prove, and for the first time in my life, I feared nothing. In a body born with no arms or legs, I was finally at peace in my own skin.

Even facing my thirty-fifth birthday did not seem to scare me. I knew that my life was not winding down but speeding up to a level that filled me with excitement. I felt that good things were ahead, and I was determined to go get them. That is what this book is all about. After years of insecurity and doubt, I had finally learned the truth of my identity. Through faith, I had accepted myself as complete. With nothing and no one holding me back, I decided to live as fully as God had intended on the day I was born. Surrounding myself with love, I began the next step of my journey.

God does not hand our dreams to us on a silver platter. Instead, He gives us tools, and He expects us to use them. One of the tools He supplied for me is the gift of writing. One cold December afternoon in

2005, I tapped into that ability when I composed the first story in this book.

Through the years, whenever anyone asked me when I was going to write a book about my life, my stomach would knot up in fear. I couldn't imagine how I would be able to maintain the integrity of my truth without imposing on anyone else's. In writing the story "I Was Born This Way," I found my way. I realized that my story was rich enough to stand alone. Shying away from standing out was no longer as important as sharing my faith. In this book, I disclose myself by focusing on the moments and the beliefs that have shaped my life. The first part of the book tells my story. The second part, which will hopefully inspire and encourage readers, provides insight into my values and beliefs.

This book is the story of how God created a path that led me out of confusion and uncertainty. Although my journey is far from over, I have now reached a plateau of divine contentment. From this vantage point, all things are possible. It is my hope that in the pages of this book, you will begin to find your own magnificent view of life.

Part One: My Story

I Was Born This Way

IT IS AMAZING WHAT YOU can see at Target stores at Christmastime. Shoppers try desperately to find the right gifts for loved ones. Elderly men are people-watch on the benches out front.

Children's faces glow at what must seem like never-ending walls of toys. Lots of people complain about this time of year. The crowds and traffic appear overwhelming to them, I guess.

Personally, I love it. Every year, I can't wait for the opportunity to see the stores and houses lit up. I can't wait to see children brimming with anticipation and excitement. I can't wait to hear the music that celebrates the birth of the Lord Jesus.

Today at Target, I experienced another thing I love about Christmas. When stores overflow with people, communication tends to take place between shoppers more than usual.

You can't help but talk to your neighbor when you have been standing in line with them for ten minutes. My neighbor today was a dark-haired little girl with big brown eyes. She was seated in her mother's shopping cart when she noticed me behind her. Much to her mother's dismay, she could not stop staring at me. Given that I now have thirty-five years of handling this kind of situation, I felt perfectly comfortable striking up a conversation. She said her name was Halley. After reciting her wish list for Santa, she asked me quickly before her mother finished at the register, "What happened to you?" I answered, "I was born this way." Like most children her age, Halley looked puzzled at my statement. I'm sure her mother did her best to explain it on the way home.

On December 8, 1970, my parents, Charlie and Gloria Wetherbee, expected to bring home the ultimate Christmas gift to my older sister, Dana. They looked forward to the arrival of a healthy baby girl or boy. Back then, doctors didn't run the tests that seem so standard today. Not only were my parents unaware that I was going to be a girl, they also did not know that I was going to be born physically disabled.

I was born with what is officially termed quadrilateral tetra-amelia. However, it is easier just to say I was born with no arms or legs. I cannot use prosthetic limbs because I have no partial limbs to which they could attach. I use a power wheelchair that I steer with my shoulder. I write with a pen in my mouth and type with a dowel stick. Out of necessity and confusion, I began communicating with God at five years old. At thirteen, I accepted His Son as my Savior. I've often said that if I were to ever write an autobiography, I would title it after the sentence I have spoken more than any other in my life: "I was born this way."

Recently, that sentence has taken on new meaning for me. I have come to realize that the Lord blessed me with a resilience that is truly remarkable. I used to think that it was wrong, if not downright arrogant, to acknowledge my inner strength. I saw glimpses of it when healing from a broken heart or when I was able to bounce back from a disappointment, but I never allowed myself to affirm it until I came to truly understand its source.

The ability to live our lives to the fullest despite overwhelming circumstances is a gift from God. It does not come from us. The joy in being part of a holiday crowd, the strength to make peace with past mistakes, and the love it takes to forgive yourself and others all come from our Lord. These gifts are not ours to boast about, but they are ours to use. The attitude we choose to adopt at any given moment is our responsibility. He gives us the ability, but we make the choice.

My wish is for everyone to see this for themselves. I believe that if we claim to know God, it is our responsibility to use and share every bit of joy, love, and strength we can muster up each day. God knew I would need these attributes to navigate this life He has given me.

I am strong. I am resilient. I was born this way, and so were you.

I'll Be Your Arms and Legs

"DON'T WORRY, ALLISON. I'LL BE your arms and legs for you."
I read those words for the first time as a teenager. My sister Dana had
spoken them to me when I was an infant. When my mother decided
to write a book in the late 1980s, she included Dana's words in the
chapter about my birth. In an attempt to protect me from the grief that
surrounded my entry into this world, no one told me of the despair my
disability had caused for my family. My heart pounded as I read and
learned about the first days and weeks of my life.

Dana was waiting at home with our mother's parents. My sister was
only six years old when I was born, and she was still adjusting to major
life changes. About a year and a half earlier, our mother met my father in
the summer of 1969. They were married six months later, and just days
before Dana was to start first grade, Mom and Dad made the decision
to move to the town that would become our home, Camden, Alabama. I
was born almost eleven months to the day after my parents were married.
Dana was at home expecting a gift in the form of a new baby that would
bring happiness and stability to her new family and surroundings.

My mother was still heavily medicated when the doctor came to my father in the waiting room. No other family members had arrived at the hospital yet. My father stood alone as he saw the troubled look on the doctor's face and heard the words, "You have a beautiful little girl, but I am so sorry to tell you that something went wrong. She has no arms or legs."

My mother had been under anesthesia when I was delivered; she didn't know anything was wrong until my father came to her room. Nine months of anticipation and dreams were shattered in that one unimaginable moment.

My parents had considered the name Susan for a baby girl. However, on the way to the hospital, my mother asked my father, "What do you think about the name Allison?" After I was born, my father had the foresight to realize that I might someday use my mouth to write. In an attempt to reduce the amount of effort that a longer name would require, he made the decision to give me no middle name.

I was an otherwise healthy infant. All of my internal organs functioned properly, and I responded to stimuli as any other baby would. The doctor said my cry was very strong. In the hospital nursery, my father saw me before my mother did. What he said when he came back to my mother's room became an amusing part of my birth story. He looked at my mother and excitedly exclaimed, "She's so beautiful! She looks just like me!"

When my parents saw me for the first time together, they laid me on my mother's hospital bed, unwrapped my blanket, and looked at every inch of my tiny body with awe. I weighed less than four pounds and measured around ten inches long. Where arms would have been, my shoulders were smooth. On the right side of my bottom, there was a small indentation similar to a belly button. On the left side there was a small round ball of tissue where my leg had started to grow. As a child,

I affectionately named that place on my hip "little leg." Although I have been blonde all of my life, I was born with a full head of jet black hair.

My mother says that the shock my family endured when I was born was eased only by the joy they found in their baby girl. I had big blue eyes, and I cooed at everything. I was a happy baby who rarely cried. In the weeks following my birth, my parents struggled with the questions of why and how my disability could have occurred. They were left with no answers until many years later. When I was a teenager, we learned that my disability was most likely caused by a medication called Bendectin that my mother had been given for nausea early in her pregnancy with me. My family did not pursue any legal recourse; it was enough of a relief knowing what caused my disability although from the beginning our focus was never on the cause.

My parents say that they made the decision early on to proceed with life as usual. Dana often sobbed as she gazed down on me in my crib and promised to help me. She could not understand why my body was not whole.

Each member of my family tells me that they found joy and healing in a baby who seemed to shine with eagerness to begin each new day. I take comfort in the knowledge that even from day one, it appeared to all that I was happy to have been born.

Why?

"WILL I BE ABLE TO run track like Dana when I get big?" I remember sitting on the den floor of our trailer and asking my dad this question. Though the house we lived in when I was born was fairly large, my parents decided to build another one to better accommodate my needs. The trailer became our refuge for one year as the "big house" was being built. It was in the trailer that I had to learn many hard facts of life.

"I just don't know, Pooh. We'll have to see." What could you say to a five-year-old girl who was just discovering for herself how different her body was from everyone else's? I remember having to work up the nerve to even ask my question in the first place. I was frightened as to what type of answer I might receive. Being Alabama's March of Dimes child the year before had exposed me to the fact that I was different from everyone else, but I just could not figure out the extent of my differences. Most of the time, it seemed as if there was nothing I could not do. I was still small enough that friends my own age were able to carry me around and play with me, so I rarely felt left out of anything.

When you're born with a disability, you don't realize the extent of your differences until they are pointed out to you. My differences first stared me in the face when I found I wasn't able to sit in the swings on the playground like the other kids. It also hit me hard when I realized that my parents were still feeding me as if I were a baby. I remember comparing my body to Sesame Street's Big Bird. I was amazed at how big his hands and feet were, and I imagined myself with limbs that size.

Trying to comprehend the magnitude of my physical differences overwhelmed me as a child. I knew I was born different, but the thought of living that way forever was appalling to me. It made me feel physically sick whenever I tried to understand the permanence of my situation. I would tell myself, "It's okay. It's not real. It won't be this way for long." I somehow knew inside this was not true, but it was the only way I could escape my reality. I could tell that even adults could not seem to wrap their minds around the situation. How on earth could a child grasp the enormity of it?

Every week, my preacher and my Sunday school teachers taught me that God was in ultimate control. Back then, I envisioned God as a trustworthy and kind parental figure. I never questioned His existence. I don't know how to explain it other than to say that I have felt His presence within me for as long as I can remember. I knew He was there and able to hear me. On the same night that I asked my dad if I would ever be able to run, I began my lifelong communication with God. I begged Him to tell me or show me why I was born so different. I remember crying in my bed while I asked, "Why did it have to be me?" I was smart enough to realize that my disability could have happened to anyone; any child could have been born the way I was. But for some reason, it wasn't any other child. It was me. At five years old, I just wanted to know why.

Nothing But the Best

ASK ME WHAT IT IS like to have been born disabled, and I can tell you pretty much all you ever wanted to know, but ask me what it is like to be the parent of a child born disabled, and I can only guess. As hard as I have tried, I can never fully grasp it. The fact is, we never completely understand what any situation is like for someone else unless we have lived something similar ourselves. My parents received no hint that I was going to be disabled. My mother already had one child, my sister Dana. My mom gained less weight with her second pregnancy, but it seemed normal otherwise. The adjustments my parents had to make, especially in the first couple of years of my life, seem unfathomable to me.

By the time I was six years old, I was an experienced traveler. Twice, sometimes three times a year, my parents would take me to Grand Rapids, Michigan, to a clinic that specialized in amputee services. It was there that I was fitted with my first walker. The device consisted of two metal legs attached to a plastered bucket seat. Seated in the bucket, I could walk by swaying my body from side to side. I was too young to remember the first time I used a walker, but I definitely remember using the device as I got older. The walkers had to be readjusted every few months to accommodate the changes in my weight, so every few months my parents took me to Michigan.

My walkers gave me my first taste of independence. They allowed me to stand upright for the first time. Without them, my only means of independent mobility was to roll around on the floor. By the time I was six years old, however, I could no longer keep my balance in walkers. I had simply outgrown them, and I often fell over. Letting them go was very difficult for me, and I remember stubbornly attempting to walk without falling. This stubbornness earned me a permanent scar on my forehead when I fell against the corner of my sister's metal bed. Eventually, even I saw that the walkers had become too dangerous, and I reluctantly let them go.

My parents began investigating the next level of independence, a power wheelchair. I was eight years old when my dad found a place that sold and modified the appliances in a nearby town. Figuring out how I would operate the chair became a full-time task. The controls had to be mounted where I could reach them. After much deliberation, we decided that I would use my right shoulder to manipulate the buttons.

The memory of being placed in my first electric wheelchair will stick with me forever. As my parents and I left the store to go home, I crossed the parking lot on my own, fully believing that nothing in life could stop me. For the first time, I could go almost anywhere I wanted without help or restrictions. That day was one of the best days of my childhood.

Whenever I'm asked why we went all the way to Michigan several times every year for six years or why we spent so much time looking for a wheelchair, my answer is always the same. It is the same answer I give whenever I am asked why my parents went to such lengths for me. The answer is because it was what was best for me.

There are probably hundreds of examples I could give of my parents doing whatever it took to make sure I received the best of whatever was needed. They gave me access to the best services, the best equipment, and the best care. The truly remarkable thing is that I believe both of my sisters would say my parents provided the same for them as well. Even though I may never fully comprehend the complexities of parenting a disabled child, I do know that my parents could always be depended upon to provide me with nothing but the best.

My Baby

OUR GOOD NEWS HAD TO stay secret for a while. Dana and I had rarely seen such pure joy on our parents faces as when they explained to us what to expect. We knew that this was a dream they had been trying to attain for years. By the time it came true, it was our dream as well. On the way to church one Sunday morning, I remember my mother saying, "Now don't forget, Allison. We're not telling everyone just yet."

The first person I saw that morning was our preacher. I don't remember which of my parents carried me up the steps toward him, but I do remember holding in my uncontainable happiness as long as my six-year-old body could. It took about ten seconds for me to loudly blurt out, "We're gonna have a baby!" All three members of my family giggled a simultaneous, "Shhhh, Allison!" but it was too late. I was more excited than I had ever been about anything in my life. I wanted the whole world to know that our baby was coming and that I was going to be a big sister.

When we learned the baby was a girl, we began planning. We started buying clothes, and Dad painted her room pale yellow. I "helped" with everything. Until the room was redone years later, I could always find the one spot I had painted while sitting in my wheelchair with a small brush in my mouth.

My mind stayed busy with anticipation throughout those long months. I could not wait for my sister to be born. A lot of children feel jealousy at the thought of a new baby in the family, but I never remember feeling that way. I had been given so much attention from all directions in my six short years that I was ready for the spotlight to shine somewhere else. I was actually ready for someone else to be the baby.

At that time, three dolls were my constant companions. I gave them names, dressed them with my mouth, and talked to them as if they were real. Collie McDale, my favorite, and David and Elizabeth were the first recipients of my developing caretaker personality. I remember feeling proud that I was responsible for the care of my three "babies." It gave me a sense of being needed, something I didn't feel very often. Because I was beginning to feel the emotional toll of my physical dependence on others, I looked forward to anything that would counteract that guilt. In the months before the baby was born, I delighted in the promise of having a little sister whom I could care for and love.

She finally came early one April morning. I rolled straight out of my bed onto the floor when I heard Dana's excited voice ask, "Is it time?" She and I waited at the house for the sun to rise and for the phone to ring. Just before a family friend was to pick us up for school, we got the call from Dad. Megan had been born. Our family of four welcomed its fifth and final little member.

The hospital did not allow children my age inside to see the newborns. That night, Dana walked through the front door of the hospital while Dad carried me around to the outside window of Mom's room. I remember laughing as Dad's hands passed me through the window to Dana's.

Sitting beside Mom in the bed, I touched Megan for the first time by kissing her warm, soft forehead. She was the most beautiful thing I had ever seen. I whispered, "Hi, baby." At that moment, I fell in love for the very first time. As far as I was concerned, Megan was my baby, and she always would be.

Magic

So many things have changed in the world during my lifetime. Cell phones and Internet were unknown when I was a child. One of the saddest phenomena of the last thirty years is the child with no imagination. The magic that children were once allowed to indulge in has been stolen by an endless array of technology. Reality shows and text messaging have replaced make-believe. I believe that those of us fortunate enough to remember the wonder of childhood are truly blessed.

I vividly remember riding a large quarter horse colored deep reddish brown. He was named for the straight, solid white blaze that covered his face. Blaze belonged to my father's brother, Ed, and his wife. He lived on forty acres of land that my family affectionately called The Place. My dad or my uncle would perch me in the saddle between his arms as Blaze took slow strides on lazy Sunday afternoons. In my five-year-old imagination, Blaze was my wild stallion, forever devoted to his Indian Princess owner. I whispered commands to take me places I had never seen, and he obeyed. In my dreams, Blaze magically understood my need to feel free from the confines of my reality, and he granted that wish every chance he got.

Riding the clouds as a nine-year-old had the same effect on me as Blaze had had. At times, my flight was slow and deliberate, but usually I soared at record speed as I wove through trees and traffic. I floated on air as a bird looking down on everyone below, far away from all the conflict and confusion of childhood. This is how it felt to ride in the bunk bed above the driver's seat in my family's Winnebago with my face pressed against the cold window. With the 1970s music of Charlie Daniels and Kenny Rogers playing in the background, I watched the tops of cars pass us on the interstate and wondered where they were going. When I knew it would take a while for us to reach our destination, I used my mouth to close the curtains that separated the bed from the rest of the vehicle. Our family vacation would then transform for me into a journey through a land where little girls could learn to fly.

Visiting my mother's family in a nearby town every Saturday also held magical moments. Each week I looked forward to playing with cousins and friends who were simultaneously rambunctious and protective of me. I was tossed around like a football by neighborhood boys, but at the end of the day, I always knew I was well cared for. Those days were full of adventure, laughter, and good food. During football season, I learned to pledge allegiance to my family's beloved college team by yelling at the television as loudly as I could, "Roll Tide!" When Alabama won, a part of me went home convinced that my cheering had somehow helped the cause.

Small-town life has its own unique pleasures, and I found my share of them. In my hometown there is a stretch of road behind the Baptist church known as Cemetery Hill. If you hit the top of this hill at just the right speed, gravity lets go of you for about three seconds. Given that the nearest roller coaster is four hours away, Cemetery Hill has served its purpose for many kids for many years. For me, however, it held even greater meaning.

I considered this rarely traveled road located only a block from our house the best playground on earth. Both sides of it were thick with kudzu-covered trees that seemed full of mystery and danger. Because of the woods, sunlight never hit the hill, which added to its mystique.

At the bottom of the hill, an old, dilapidated house was nestled far back in the trees. I named it the Haunted Huntin' House. My idea of fun was to see how close I could get to the house before screaming out in fear. Each day, my babysitter, Emily, would push me in my stroller a little closer to the house, but I never made it to the porch.

I also made a game out of talking Emily into sitting me in my little red wagon, pulling me to the top of the hill, and turning me loose. The faster we could make that wagon go, the happier I was. I always landed just fine, but when my mom found out what we were doing, she wasn't too thrilled. My family has always remembered with amusement Emily's attempt to reassure her. "I know Allison is alright, Mrs. Wetherbee, before I even get to her. She giggles so hard that the kudzu wiggles."

Our dreams do not have to diminish just because we grow up; they can become bigger than our childhood imaginations ever conceived. Much of what I do as an adult I never dreamed would be possible as a child. Back then, my imagination was my escape, not only from my physical limitations, but also from a future that seemed so uncertain. However, the future that I was so afraid to face has been full of magic and dreams come true. The wonder of life never has to end. If we are brave enough, we can still fly above what others say is hopeless.

Happy Camper: Part One

ACCORDING TO MY MOM, I came home one day from second grade with a plan. I had gotten my attendant to stuff my backpack full of important information that I had been given at school, and I kept exclaiming, "I want to go to Girl Scout camp!" I was ready to go right then. The camp I was so excited about would not accept me without a full-time caretaker to see to my needs. Going to camp with my mom or an attendant just didn't sit right with the free-spirited child that I was. I wanted to go to camp by myself just like everybody else, but in the long run, none of that really mattered. God had better plans in mind anyway.

Through a hometown friend, we found Easter Seals Camp ASCCA. Back then, the acronym stood for Alabama's Society for Crippled Children and Adults. In an effort to further society's understanding of the disabled, it was renamed Alabama's Special Camp for Children and Adults in the 1980s. I remember playing in our backyard plastic pool when Mom asked me how I would feel about attending a camp where all of the children would be handicapped. Because we lived in a small community where I attended "regular" classes in school, I had rarely seen other disabled children. I remember my concern that I would not be with my friends from school, but I agreed to try the camp anyway. This would prove to be one of the best decisions my parents and I ever made, and I'm convinced that God's hand was directing it all.

The summer before third grade, I went to camp for the first time. The session I attended was for children between the ages of six and ten. The length of the two-week stay caused a great deal of anxiety for my parents. Other than weekly overnight stays with my grandmother, this would be the first time I was away from home more than one night. I remember feeling scared myself, but I hid my fears and told myself to be a big girl. I didn't cry until my counselor pushed me in my stroller away from my parents. As I peeped back behind me, I whispered to them, "Bye-bye."

During my first visit to camp, I didn't have time to get homesick. I was kept busy with arts and crafts, canoeing, and plenty of singing. I loved everything about it, especially the people that I befriended.

My first time at camp wasn't quite as easy on my parents as it was on me. Back then, the phone system at Camp ASCCA wasn't as sophisticated it is today. When someone called, every phone on the campus rang, including the ones at the administrator's and the director's houses. So, each time Mrs. Wetherbee called to check on Allison, everyone knew it! I don't remember this myself, but my mom tells with amusement that after about four nights of her calls, I told her I was having fun and that she didn't need to keep calling back because it was embarrassing me!

Forever Friends

MY FIRST CAMP COUNSELOR, DONETTE Dunagan Mullinix, sat me down on the bathroom floor so we would have plenty of reading light. She held a large book that seemed as big as I was when she opened it. As she began to read, I remember feeling very nervous. I was only seven at the time, but I sensed bad news coming. Donette was attempting to answer a question I had asked her earlier that day. Being the good counselor that she was, she wanted to make sure the information she gave me was accurate. My question was, "What is muscular dystrophy (MD)?" I wasn't asking on my own behalf. I was asking because my new best friend knew she had MD, but she didn't know how to explain it to me. We had met just a few days earlier. Her name was Latonya, and she was almost six years old.

As Donette read, I learned that Latonya would gradually lose all use of her muscles. I also learned that there was no cure for MD and that Latonya's life would almost certainly end prematurely due to the effects of the disease. I never spoke to Latonya about what I read from Donette's book, but it didn't take me long to realize that my friend already knew her fate. I believe children can sense things even when they don't have the words to explain them.

From the moment I discovered what MD was, my idea of time changed. I no longer enjoyed the child's luxury of thinking that all things in this life would go on forever. I had a feeling of urgency for the first time. I felt as if Latonya and I needed to have as much fun as possible in the time we had left at camp. That was the goal, and we reached it as often as two little girls could.

Latonya and I ate our meals together, went swimming together, and had overnight parties as frequently as our counselors would let us. We piled up in each other's beds to talk and giggle for hours. Just like other little girls, we took turns brushing each other's hair. Latonya didn't think it was gross that I had to put the brush in my mouth, and I didn't think it was odd that she occasionally lost her balance and fell over.

We referred to our differences as handicaps back then, and we spoke about them openly. For the first time, I had a friend to whom I could talk about my disability without shame or embarrassment. When I was with Latonya, I didn't have to worry about trying to be "normal." We were like two pieces of a puzzle. We could relax when we were together, because we fit.

Each summer I looked forward to seeing Latonya at Camp ASCCA. Slowly, bit by bit as the years passed, I watched time steal Latonya's ability to walk. I was seventeen the last time I saw her. By that time, she was using a brace to hold her posture straight, and she wasn't able to move with much freedom, but she still came to camp every summer. Each time I saw her, she had a huge smile on her face, because, as she told me once, "Camp ASCCA is my favorite place in the world to be."

My last contact with Latonya came in the form of a letter a year later. The post date on it is July 12, 1989. I will continue to keep it safely in my Bible for the rest of my life. I can tell it took a lot of energy for her to compose, because by the end of the three pages, her script becomes hard to read. Latonya wrote, "I wish you lived closer to me. I think it would help if I had someone I could talk to who understands all of my problems." I wrote her back several times, but I never heard from her again.

Latonya touched my soul in such a way that still influences me. I believe with all my heart that one day we will see each other again and that when we do, we will enjoy a privilege that I have never had and that Latonya lost as an eight-year-old child: we will stand upright and embrace.

A few months after I wrote "Forever Friends," my mom called to say she had seen an obituary that she would save for me. She wasn't sure if it was Latonya's, but as she read the newspaper clipping over the phone, I knew it announced my friend's death. Latonya had passed away the week before Thanksgiving 2007. For many reasons, her life had a huge impact on mine, and I will always be grateful to her for being my friend. I love you, Latonya, and I can't wait to see you again someday.

The Mistake

MY NURSE, KATIE, LIGHTLY TAPPED on my hospital room door to check on me for the third time. On this occasion, she didn't offer me a sleeping aid or a sip of water. Instead, she just hugged me and sat with me for a few minutes while I cried. She had the mid-1980s Olivia Newton-John hairstyle and didn't wear much makeup. I remember Katie so well, because she kept me company during one of the most frightening nights of my life. The following day, surgeons at Children's Hospital in Boston would try to correct the curvature in my spine. My parents had gone to their motel room to rest up for an operation that we were told could last ten hours or more. I had strongly assured them that I would be just fine by myself that night. Even though I was only thirteen years old, I had already learned how to hold back my tears very well.

When Katie left the room, I began the final stretch of the ongoing conversation I had been having with God since learning I would need surgery. I had begun questioning God when I was five. At eight years of age, I begged Him to give me arms and legs. By thirteen, I was settling into the realization that my disability was permanent. The emotional toll of adjusting to that reality was so great that no words can accurately describe it. Like every other preadolescent girl, I had images of getting married someday and having children. Unlike other girls, though, my imagination was clouded with unanswerable questions. What would I look like as a bride in a wheelchair? How would I hold my children? Who could ever fall in love with me anyway? And the most consuming question of all was how a loving and kind God could let me be born and live like this in the first place. In the months prior to the surgery, I had come to the only sensible conclusion I could find to this question: I came to believe that I must have been God's one mistake.

When I told my family and friends good-bye as my parents and I left for Boston, I fully believed I would not be coming home. In my mind, I had decided that God was going to let me die and thus solve the mistake He had made when He created me. My dad had looked all over the country for a doctor experienced with this type of operation on a patient with my disabilities. He found only one. That fact in and of itself left me totally convinced that the odds were against my survival.

Alone in my hospital bed, I made my peace with God that night. In my childlike language, I let Him know that I wasn't angry. I remember actually saying the words, "It's okay if you want to take me. I won't be mad." I also promised that if He chose for me to live, I would do my best with the life He had given me.

When I woke up the next morning, I was eerily calm. My memories of those hours are very vivid. My parents and I watched *The Dukes of Hazard* while we waited for the nurses to come and take me to the operating room. I didn't cry when they pulled my bed away from my parents, but I did weep when a nurse told me to breathe in an anesthesia that smelled like bananas. When I woke up fourteen hours later, my mom was the first thing I saw. I don't remember her words to me, but she does. She asked, "How did it go, Allison?" I answered, "Better than I thought it would." She had no idea just how honest my reply was!

The operation itself, as well as my recovery, had more complications than anyone predicted. A couple of days following the surgery, doctors had to drain fluid from one of my lungs after it collapsed, and they struggled to keep the other lung from collapsing. During my painful and heavily medicated recovery, I was fascinated by the tricks my eyes played on me. I often thought I saw the walls breathe!

As I became more alert with each passing day, I felt more alive than ever. I knew in my heart that God wanted me to live. When my parents and I finally left the hospital, I shouted with joy for the first time in my young life. As I grew older, I often wondered what my purpose was on this planet. But, on that sunny day in Boston I felt God looking down on me. It was then that I knew beyond any doubt that He never creates mistakes, not even one.

He Loves You, Sweetheart

IN THE SUMMER OF 1984, I could not sit up in my chair for longer than a couple of hours. I had spent the better part of two months flat on my back on our den sofa. I was stiff with physical pain and boredom, but I also had a mission that kept my thirteen-year-old mind occupied and focused. My goal was to reach a level of recovery from surgery sufficient to allow me to attend summer camp. I had the surgery in April, and I wanted to be at Camp ASCCA by June.

I promised worried friends that nothing would stop me from attending camp. For the first time in a couple of years, I knew in my soul that God intended for me to live. I knew that my being born had not been a mistake. I wanted nothing more in life that summer than to be reminded of how it felt to be free.

At Camp ASCCA, a camp designed to meet the needs of the disabled, I was free. There were no barriers anywhere. I could watch the sun rise or set over Lake Martin and play in the water when the sky's colors had faded. I could be entranced by the sight of thousands of fireflies above a paved nature trail or spend hours talking to a friend I had made years before.

My disability led to my becoming very mature for my age, because I had not had the luxury of a carefree childhood. Every summer, the college-aged staff at camp delighted in taking me under their wing. On most levels, I was able to relate to them. I offered them encouragement and friendship. The priceless gifts they gave me in return have stayed with me throughout my life. In their presence, I found total acceptance and belonging.

Understandably, my excitement was uncontainable that summer when I was able to make it to camp despite the concerns of my parents and doctors. Because sitting up for too long caused me intense pain, I was forced to spend a large amount of time in bed. However, my confinement didn't seem to matter much to me. My mission was complete, and it didn't take me long to discover that my ambition to get to camp that summer was also in God's plan.

People I had known for years came by to visit with me throughout the summer while I was at camp because they knew about my recent surgery. Two of those old friends had been counselors my first year at camp. I had always known Billy Windham as a tough character who knew how to set me straight whenever I acted up as a child. All it took was a particular look to get my attention. I also have a sweet memory of Billy holding me tight when I was seven years old as I cried on his shoulder for reasons I can't remember. I knew Ann Cope as a kind and gentle girl with a beautiful smile. Given that I was so young when I met them, I had not developed a truly close friendship with either of them, but they were the kind of friends who left me unable to remember a time when I didn't know them. It was as if they were just always there. When they walked into my room one afternoon that summer, I was perfectly comfortable and glad to see them.

Billy began the conversation with the declaration that he and Ann felt as if they had been led to camp that day just to visit me. When I questioned what he meant by the word "led," Billy explained, "I believe God wants us to talk to you about something. We believe that He wants us to talk to you about Jesus." When they asked if I knew the Son of God, I let them know that I had been going to church with my family all of my life.

I knew in my soul that Billy's next words came straight from God. He asked, "Do you know that God has a plan and a purpose for you and that there's a reason why you're here?" Billy picked me up as he had done so many times in my young life and held me close to him. He lifted my chin so that I was positioned to look straight into his eyes when he said, "God loves you, Allison. It was not a mistake that you were born like this. He loves you, sweetheart."

Billy placed me into my wheelchair and asked if I knew that I needed a Savior. What I knew, that they did not, was that I had been questioning God for years. I felt the burden of that wrong. I acknowledged to them that I was in need of forgiveness and that my relationship with God needed to be made right. They asked for my permission to pray with me. When I said yes, Billy and Ann wrapped their arms around me. Billy kept his hand tight on the back of my head as he bowed his forehead against mine. He then led me through the prayer of accepting Christ into my heart.

In that moment in time, all of my questions were answered, and the answer was Jesus, the Son of God. I was saved not by my own doing but by God's will. God planned for me to be born with no arms or legs. God planned my need for Him, and God planned for me to be in that bed on that afternoon at Camp ASCCA to receive His message of salvation and love through the two friends whom He had led to me. I was saved, and I never questioned God again.

Set Me Free

AT FOUR YEARS OLD, I thought I knew a woman named Delta Dawn. In my mind, she was a beautiful, raven-haired woman who traveled the streets of Camden. The songwriters who had vividly crafted this character in Tanya Tucker's hit song lit a fire in my soul and began my lifelong love affair with music.

"Sing for us, Allison," Dana would say, as she placed me in the middle of the living room or on the top of our stereo cabinet. While she and her friends lined up in front of me, I would prepare to put on a show. I shook my head and scooted on my bottom to the beat of the songs I sang as loud as my little lungs would let me. In a tiny, angelic voice, I belted out my favorites: "Delta Dawn," "Cotton Fields Back Home," and "Love Potion #9." I was thrilled to entertain "the big girls," and they ate up every minute of it.

I got Megan to learn almost every word of the *Grease* soundtrack when she was only five. I was the eleven-year-old director of our version of the movie, but Megan was primed to be the star. Hours went by each afternoon as we choreographed dance steps and poses to accompany the songs. By the opening night of our grand production, we were ready.

When the audience—our family—flocked to the stage—my bedroom—Megan's snaggletoothed version of "Hopelessly Devoted" melted hearts.

As I grew older, music became more than just a source of pleasure and fun for me. By the time I was a teenager, music had become a healing balm to be applied whenever I felt alone or misunderstood. In the invention of the Walkman, I found a safe harbor at the end of each day. I stored at least a dozen cassette tapes under the pillows of my bed at all times so that I would have a choice of who sang me to sleep. Certain troubles called for certain songs, and I knew how to match the music to my moods.

Whenever I felt sadness I had no desire to conquer, Hank Williams Sr. never let me down. When my teenaged woes needed alleviation, Hank Williams Jr. and Lynyrd Skynyrd saved the day. Bruce Springsteen wouldn't let me give up on my dreams, and Steve Earle reminded me things could always be worse. These artists befriended me through their music. I listened to their words, and thank goodness they never steered me wrong. They kept me company as I lay in the dark each night wondering what the next day would hold. I'd fall asleep knowing that whatever the future brought, it would be a little easier with their help.

I ended up buying John Mellencamp's album *Scarecrow* three separate times because I wore out one copy after another. With the song, "Minutes To Memories," he told me, a fourteen-year-old girl with no arms or legs, "You are young and you are the future, so suck it up, tough it out, and be the best you can." This became an internal mantra to repeat whenever I felt like giving up during my teen years.

As the girl whom everyone called an inspiration, I found my own inspiration through music. It was the soothing noise that filtered out the background drama of my life. When I reached my twenties, my need for music changed. I no longer depended on it as my only source of lasting comfort, but I never forgot how important the music, and the artists who created it, had been to me. When I began composing music in college, lyrics that expressed my gratitude naturally emerged:

I found comfort in your voice just like a mother's prayer,
And someday I will thank you, somehow, somewhere.
They say that we get just what we deserve,
But on days like today, it feels so much worse!
Give me my confirmation, a little reason to still believe.
Cut through the disillusion, and let the music set me free.

Memories of England

AT A BUS STOP IN England, I said good-bye to a handful of beautiful personalities who had come into my life only briefly but would live in my memory forever. We were all on our way to catch our plane rides back home. The first to say good-bye were Bostonians, David and Raymond. David was one of the disabled Americans chosen by Rotary International to attend an all expenses paid trip to England for two weeks. Raymond, David's cousin, had come along as his helper. Chosen through my connection with Camp ASCCA, I was the second American attendee.

It was a breezy July in 1985, and I was a rambunctious fourteen-year-old. I had already been through so much in my short life that sixteen-year-old Raymond recognized me as an old soul one night as we sat together in the middle of an English rose garden. Raymond had developed his own old soul on the streets of Boston. Our backgrounds held absolutely nothing in common, but we realized a common link the moment we met. In totally different circumstances, we had each grown up fast and faced situations that would have left most adults dumbfounded. We spent hours in mature conversation about racial stereotypes and laughed, like the children we were, at each other's accents. At that bus station,

Raymond tearfully told me good-bye with a soft kiss on the cheek and a whisper, "Stay the way you are, Allison. Stay sweet. I won't ever forget you." Probably realizing that he would never see me again, he turned around and came back to say, "Promise me that you won't let anyone, or anything, change you." Raymond had already told me several times he was afraid that the difficulties I would surely face as I grew older would turn my heart cold. Fully understanding what he was asking of me, I promised as I watched Raymond walk away for good.

Connor, from Northern Ireland, made his good-bye brief. Probably because Connor and I had already bonded more than we ever should have, there was no need for a drawn out farewell scene. Connor was in his early twenties, which made him quite a bit older than me. He made his living as a newspaper photographer in Northern Ireland and had the bloody stories to prove it. He had gotten his ticket for this Rotary International trip through a disabled friend whom he was accompanying.

Connor was the definition of spontaneity and compulsivity. He drank too much every night and kept up an active conversation with whomever happened to be nearby. Connor also flirted a lot, especially when the Guinness kicked in. As one of the physically strongest men in our group, he often carried me from place to place.

At the end of one night, as everyone was getting ready to leave the pub, Connor carried me out to the van that our group used for transportation. When he sat me down on the front seat, he began kissing and touching me. As the other members of our group began piling into the vehicle, I saw fingers pointing and heard comments spoken. Before Dorothy, the woman who had accompanied me on this trip, boarded the van, Connor stopped his caresses. I remember nodding and smiling at all of the concerned faces that surrounded me in an effort to assure them I was all right. The only thing that hurt was the knowledge that my first kiss had been with a drunken Irishman whom I barely knew. I regretted leaving some of my innocence in England.

Then there was dear Alistair from Scotland and sweet Wendy from England. On our last night in the UK, the entire group gathered for our last dinner and the subsequent good-bye party. I wept the whole night, knowing that these people who had captured a piece of my heart would probably be lost to me forever the next morning. Wendy was the mothering type. She kept holding me and saying, "Dear heart, Allison, nothing is supposed to last forever." She comforted me through those long hours and took me to my room right before the sun rose. I don't remember seeing her again before leaving for the bus stop.

Alistair, who was convinced that all southerners in the United States must bear some resemblance to the characters from *Gone With the Wind*, hated good-byes. He had been the big brother figure to everyone in our group. He was hotheaded and was not afraid to show that he could hold his own, but he was also gentle and protective if need be. Alistair taught me the value of my American citizenship. His fondest dream was to come to the United States, and his vision of living here dominated his conversation. His mental image of our country was primarily based on what Hollywood television programs and movies had taught him. I tried to explain the nation in more realistic terms, but Alistair was hooked on the dream. As far as he was concerned, the country that I was privileged to call home was the land of milk and honey, so I was careful to not say anything that would tarnish his dream. Alistair did not say good-bye. Instead, he ran alongside the bus as it pulled away, waving and shouting to all on board, "I will not forget you!"

I will never forget those two magical weeks in England. The scenery and the tourist attractions were breathtaking, but the people with whom I was so blessed to share this trip were its greatest treasure. The friends who touch our lives help us learn and grow. It is through the journeys we take with others that we discover ourselves and who we want to become. Good company turns good memories into unforgettable ones.

Facing Fear

My PRAYER AS AN EIGHT-YEAR-OLD girl was, "Lord, please give me arms and legs before I turn eighteen." I asked this of God from my bedroom, night after night, for several months. In my mind, ten years was plenty of time for God to accomplish the task that would eliminate my problem. My fifteen-year-old sister, Dana, was in the beginning stages of planning for college. She knew what she was going to do after high school. I did not, and by the time I was eight years old, that uncertainty was my biggest worry.

I knew that as long as I was in school my life would be predictable. My mom would get me up every morning and take me to and from school. Every summer, I would go to Camp ASCCA. There was a certain amount of comfort in this routine. As far as I was concerned, life after high school resembled the earth suddenly going flat. My wildest imagination could not take me beyond that point in time.

Around the age of fourteen, my parents and I began talking about the choices we had for my future. We didn't know what was even possible, because in the mid-1980s there were few, if any, examples of people with severe disabilities living independently. We discussed my leaving home to attend college like my sister, but we had no idea of how or even if that could be done. We had one million questions with no answers.

My biggest worry was heightened to fear with the thought that going to college was asking for far too much. I was afraid that I would be asking too much from my parents as well as from life in general. God had given me a life with no arms or legs. Who was I to ask for something out of life that seemed virtually impossible?

Starting in 1986, I worked at Easter Seals Camp ASCCA for three consecutive summers as a public relations assistant. I was fifteen that first summer, which seemed to be the age when all adults wanted to know my plans for the future. I remember feeling so frustrated at times because I didn't have definite answers to those questions. I felt a self-imposed pressure to do the right thing for all concerned. I just didn't know what the right thing was. I felt confused and afraid. One of the people at camp whom I tended to gravitate toward when troubled was Sam Hetherington.

Sam was the maintenance director at camp throughout most of the 1980s, and I was convinced that he could fix anything. He was straightforward, honest, and real. I first met him at camp when I was twelve years old. From that time on he called me "Alli Cat" and called himself my friend. When Sam said something, you knew he meant it, because his attitude left no room for doubt. Even to this day, Sam always tells me, "You are the strongest person I know." His statement feels a bit like a mountain trying to convince an anthill of its strength. As for the issue of stubbornness, I knew when I met Sam that I had met my match.

I remember psyching myself up the afternoon I decided to go talk to Sam. I had to be prepared, because not only was Sam a great listener, but he would also ask tough questions to make me confront my problem. When I got to the maintenance shop, I made up an explanation for my presence rather than just telling him that I needed to talk. Sam noticed that I was being unusually quiet. When he asked what was wrong, I unloaded all of my worries, fears, and doubts. When I finished speaking, the first thing he said was something I never forgot. He said, "Well, God gave us two ways to make a living, either with our heads or our hands. I use my hands to make my living. The way I see it, sweetheart, He didn't give you a choice." With that one amusing statement, Sam turned something that seemed so complicated into something manageable. He took what I thought was an insolvable problem and gave it a simple solution.

He asked me repeatedly what I wanted to do in life, but I couldn't give him a clear answer. I got frustrated and snapped at him, "I don't know what I want to do or should do, Sam. That's why I'm down here talking to you!" He didn't quit, though, because he understood that the first step had to come from me. I was the one who had to say what I wanted to do with my life. That basic decision was mine and mine alone.

Finally Sam said, "Look, you've already told me what everyone else thinks and says about this. All I want to know is what Allison wants. What do you want to do?" Tearing up but trying not to cry, I looked straight at Sam and said, "I want to go to college."

The Prom

I WAS RARELY THE STEREOTYPICALLY silly girl who giggled on the phone for hours. Instead, I was more of a tomboy throughout my teenage years. I enjoyed learning how to put on makeup, and I had the same dreams as most girls do, but spending hours doing things like shopping for clothes and letting my mom curl my hair was the last thing on earth I wanted to do.

I thank the Lord for that attitude in high school, because it saved me from disappointment. I didn't care that much if I didn't get asked out on dates. I had no interest in being the prettiest girl in school. I was popular; my peers always voted for me to hold a class officer seat. But being popular in school was never really that important to me. As a teenager, my interests were music, writing in my journals, and looking forward to seeing friends I had made at Camp ASCCA.

For a brief, life-defining moment during eleventh grade, the attitude that had always seen me through faltered for the first time. Peer pressure hit me in the form of the high school prom. I had absolutely no intention of going to the junior prom, despite the fact that our class was responsible for the planning and decorations. I didn't mind being involved on that level, but I wanted nothing to do with the whole "finding a prom dress and date" thing.

Then the big question started coming at me on all fronts. Everyone from classmates to family wanted to know, "Who are you going to the prom with?" My mom even suggested that I ask my cousin! Before I knew it, I was in the middle of a bad teenaged nightmare, and I couldn't wake up long enough to stop it. My only consolation was that most of my friends found themselves looking for dates also.

The quest to find a prom date began. Mom began worrying when I totally ruled out asking my cousin. My friends offered numerous suggestions during this heated battle to find the right boy. The pressure was building, and time was running out. The tissue paper and streamers were being strategically placed around the gym as I agonized over who would be brave enough to escort me on the big night. It had to be someone who wouldn't mind taking the girl who was different and who wouldn't worry about standing out in a crowd.

At seventeen years old, I still didn't feel comfortable asking someone to help feed me. I had no idea how comfortable a boy would feel about dancing with me. I didn't even have the basic answers that would get me through that night. How could I expect a self-conscious teenaged boy to muster up more composure than I could find?

Finally, just as the balloons were being blown up, a boy called. His name was Will. He was younger than I was, but that didn't matter. He had been approached by a classmate of mine to ask me, and he had agreed. The plan was to double-date, which took some pressure off, but given that this was so far out of my comfort zone, I was terrified. I had recovered from major back surgery with life-threatening complications at thirteen. At fourteen, I had flown overseas to stay in England for two weeks without a family member. I had stayed away from home for weeks at a time at Camp ASCCA starting at seven years old. But on the night of the junior prom, I feverishly prayed for God to give me the fortitude to not faint before my date arrived at my house!

As I counted the number of hours before the whole thing would be over, my mom stuffed me into a red taffeta dress that she had made just for this occasion. I vividly remember telling God and myself that if I could just get through that night, I could do anything. My bouffant hairdo stretched toward heaven as we left the house. It had fallen limp by the time I got home five hours later. Exhausted from worry and relieved that it was all over, I slept like a baby that night.

Will had been a perfect escort and taken everything in stride. I had survived and learned a valuable lesson. There is a reason why ducks don't stay out of the water for long: it doesn't feel right. The perfume, pearls, and hair spray were just not me at the time. Eventually, I would grow into those things to a certain extent, but as a seventeen-year-old girl, I had experienced things that had left me unable to relate to kids my own age entirely successfully. One of the social skills that I had honed by that time was the capacity to make myself fit into any group. As someone who could have easily been an outsider, I had learned how to make small talk and blend with the crowd around me; however, just because I knew how to do this didn't mean that I enjoyed it. That prom night, I learned to take comfort in knowing that there were places where I did belong and that it was not necessary to force myself to conform where I didn't. It was the very first step in the long journey of discovering that just being me was good enough. The next year, saying no to the senior prom was not a problem.

Happy Camper: Part Two

I WAS VERY QUIET DURING the drive home from Easter Seals Camp ASCCA that first summer. There was so much I wanted to tell my parents that I didn't know where to begin. I missed Donette, my first counselor, and the friends I had made. No matter how I tried, my seven-year-old language just couldn't seem to convey to anyone how much that place had touched me.

It was at camp that I had my first experience of being around a lot of people and realizing that no one was staring at me. It was the first time I had become friends with other children with disabilities at least as severe as my own. I felt complete, understood, and at ease there. I was too young to bridge the gap between my feelings toward camp and everyone else's understanding of why it meant so much to me. I saw in that first year that my home life and my time at camp were going to be two separate realities for me and that no matter how much I wanted to, I would not be able to merge them.

Over the course of the next ten years, camp became my home away from home. When I was ten years old, I begged my parents to arrange for me to stay for two consecutive sessions. That meant that I would be away from home for a month each summer until I turned fifteen in 1986, when I was asked to be a public relations assistant at camp for the next three summers. Since Camp ASCCA is open year-round, I always attended fall, winter, and spring weekend sessions also. Throughout my childhood, I was never away from camp for longer than three months at a time. It was an enormous part of my life. At the end of each summer, I would sob as I told my friends good-bye, and I counted down the days on my calendar until my return. I learned lessons and made friends there that would last a lifetime. My parents paved the way for all the accomplishments I've achieved in my life. Attending Camp ASCCA provided the spring board that allowed me to know I could achieve those goals. Even though the two worlds of home and camp seldom converged, together they made a superb team. That team made me who I am today.

When plans were set for me to go to college, I knew that my life was going to have to change. Camp ASCCA was built to serve both children and adults, but I could not see myself attend camp as a college student. I decided that the summer of 1988 would be my last season at camp. My childhood was over, and camp was where my childhood had been spent. I knew in my heart it was time to move on. I returned in the fall for one last weekend and one last good-bye. Several of my old friends were there, and I got to spend my last full day at camp doing what I thoroughly enjoyed. I made arrangements to spend the day with the Sam, the maintenance director, and his family. He fed me fried catfish the whole afternoon as we all sat on their couch watching an Alabama football game.

The last time my life at camp and my life at home came together occurred in celebration of what I considered the official end of my youth. I believed my high school graduation was my rite of passage to adulthood. The night I graduated, I had a host of loved ones in the audience patiently waiting for my name to be called. Aunts, uncles, and cousins from both sides of my family attended. A van load of people from camp, headed by my dear friend Mark Benson, cheered me on. My parents and sisters stood as close to the stage as they could get. I never expected the roar that rose in the gymnasium when my name was called. Everyone in the audience stood up, including my fellow classmates. Receiving my high school diploma was one of the most exciting moments of my life.

That night, I considered myself among the most fortunate people in the world, because I knew I was loved. I was surrounded by people who had given of themselves in so many ways for my sake. I had no idea what the future might hold, but I knew where I had come from. I had a whole world of love behind me that I would carry with me for the rest of my life. A whole world of dreams lay ahead of me, and I had been given all I needed to go chase them.

The Best Years of My Life

"I DON'T WANT CNN TO come to my high school graduation!" This is a sentence I never dreamed I would hear myself utter, but I said it to my mom as we sat in our kitchen the night before I graduated from high school. Apparently, my dad had called the CNN offices in Atlanta and asked if they would be interested in covering the graduation ceremony. Much to my surprise, the television station had agreed to attend. My motivation for rejecting the publicity was simple.

Much of my childhood had been well documented in newspapers and television; I had been Alabama's March of Dimes Child and Easter Seal's Child of the Year at four and ten years old, respectively; certain newspaper and television reporters had taken a special interest in me and featured me in several stories. By the time I was eighteen years old, I was a veteran at dealing with the media. I appreciated my Dad's enthusiasm, but getting through high school was such an ordeal that I simply wanted the milestone of graduation to remain a private affair.

I also wanted to respect the privacy of my classmates. They were the ones who had helped me through my days at school, and I shared a unique relationship with them. I had never taken special education classes. Therefore, I was graduating with the same group of kids that had attended play school with me. An attendant had gone to school with me until the sixth grade. By that time, my friends and I had grown tired of having an adult around all the time, so with my parents' permission, I began to go to school unattended with only the help of my friends.

We had grown up together, and the uniqueness of our relationship derived from the fact that they had never known life without someone like me in it. Other people reacted with a wide range of emotions to the little girl with no arms or legs. They responded with feelings that ran the gamut from fear to shock, but I could not shock the kids who had grown up with me, and they certainly did not fear me.

To them, I was just Allison. I was normal to them. I was the infant who had played next to them on baby blankets. I was the girl that they hid in sock drawers while playing hide and go seek. I was the one they loved to place in the middle of the trampoline while they circled playfully around. As our parents cringed, they would hold hands, count to three, and jump as hard as they could just to see how high they could make me fly into the air. We played hard as children. We fought and made up more than a dozen times. They wiped my tears away whenever I got hurt or embarrassed. We watched each other struggle through conflicts with teachers and algebra tests. By graduation night, we had become a team.

Along with the rest of the audience, my classmates stood and cheered as they watched me finish what we had all started together so many years before. We all knew and talked about the fact that nothing was going to be the same after that night. Many of us, including myself, were pleased with that fact. We had nothing against each other. It was just that we were ready for the change that was coming. We were ready to take the next step of our journey even though it meant separating from each other.

Many adults tried to tell me that those years would be the best of my life. Even then, I knew that was not true, and my journey since then has proven me right. My years in high school were very difficult for me. I dealt with anger, depression, and fear. Aside from the typical teenaged growing pains, I also experienced issues involving my disability. There were of course fun times with high school friends that I look back upon with fondness. One of my sweetest memories is the moment I discovered that our senior annual had been dedicated to me as a surprise gift. As I said before, we were a team.

When the night finally arrived for us to say good-bye to high school, I was ready to see it come to an end. I brimmed with fear, excitement, and determination. I could not wait to start the rest of my life. To me, my graduation was not an ending. Instead, it was a beginning to what truly would become the best years of my life.

My Last Pity Party

MY COLLEGE YEARS AT AUBURN University at Montgomery were a wonderful mixture of adventure and normalcy. I absolutely loved learning new things and having the freedom to explore the subjects that interested me the most. I maintained a high grade point average throughout my time at AUM, where I would eventually graduate with a master's degree in mental health counseling.

By the time I began college, I had already faced the most difficult inner struggles that my disability would ever force me to overcome. Without the emotional baggage that those struggles caused, I was able to develop a deeper level of identity that reached beyond my disability. I was discovering my truth beyond my physical limitations. This process was a blast at its best and messy at its worst. Mistakes were made, but lessons were learned.

College is a place where education generally goes much farther than just what is taught in the classroom. When I graduated, I emerged a determined woman who knew who she was and what she wanted in life. The pivotal moment that led to this self-assurance is one I will never forget. The lesson of it still surrounds me to this day. Its evidence can be seen in my way of life as well as in my home.

There is a motto that I see every morning as I enter my kitchen. It is written on a sign that was one of the first purchases I made for my new home in 1999. Recently, a friend of mine who was visiting pointed to this sign every time my voice reflected a certain tone. My own sign, which displays the motto "No Whining," was being used against me. My friend and I had a good laugh at the aggravation I feigned, but secretly I wished that my sign had an automatic sensor. It would be nice if it could sound an alarm anytime I'm tempted to display the most annoying behavior in the world: whining.

Even though I am clearly not above indulging in a good whine from time to time, I refuse to live in it. There are those who wallow in the sea of their complaints. They seem to be so submerged in negativity it feels as if the complaints begin to feed off each other and breed new ones. Sometimes it even seems these people would rather whine about their situations than change them.

As a disabled person, each day of my life presents unique challenges. Some of these challenges I am prepared to face, but most of them I am not. To me, the unexpected has become the norm. My life itself is fertile ground for pessimism, which I know a thing or two about. I know what it is like to have week-long whining sessions. I know how it feels to be stuck in the sadness of things I can't change. I have been so overwhelmed at times that I did not know where to even begin. Because I have been there, I also know just how much energy it takes to stay there.

Negative energy drains you like nothing else can. It's draining to spend time around negative people, and it's draining to maintain a negative outlook. I know from personal experience that it takes much more energy to look down all of the time than it does to look up. Even flowers know that it is better to face the sun than the shade. The fact is that God blessed all of creation with a will to survive. We were created with a built-in instinct to flourish. Whenever we get stuck in the darkness of negativity, we stop growing. Our emotional, physical, and spiritual lives suffer when we choose to focus on all that is lacking rather than all that is abundant. God's blessings are found in such abundance that they are immeasurable, and choosing not to see them takes work.

My last major bout with the whining, self-pitying song and dance happened in my third year of college. My last pity party was not caused by the circumstances surrounding it. It was caused by me and my own attitude. The problems I faced at that juncture have recurred several times since then on an even larger scale. The difference in my reactions then and now can be credited to the wisdom of a lesson learned.

I was lying in bed talking with God as I had done hundreds of times. I was telling Him that if I just had arms and legs, I would be happy. I would not have to deal with certain problems. I would be able to take care of myself and not have to depend on anyone. Over and over, I said, "If I just had arms and legs, I would be happy."

All of a sudden, a thought came to me that I had never previously considered: *everyone I knew had two good arms and two good legs, and not one of them was truly happy.* Every one of them longed for something more than what they had. They had arms and legs, but not one of them was totally satisfied and content. I could come to only one conclusion— peace and happiness do not depend on circumstance. This realization rocked my world, and I have not been the same since.

What I know now is that if I am unhappy for any considerable amount of time, it is no one's fault but mine. Since that epiphany in 1991, I know that I can no longer blame anyone or anything for my emotional upset. Even the absence of limbs is not an excuse to whine, because now I know that having a satisfied heart has nothing to do with circumstances. Choices are made every moment of every day. I can choose for my soul to be at peace, or I can choose for it to be at war. The choice is made according to what I choose to focus on, and that is completely up to me.

I now make a conscious effort to surround myself with reminders of this fact. My "No Whining" sign has good company. Two other signs in my home assist me in remembering my lesson. The one above my kitchen sink reads, *"It's a Wonderful Life,"* commemorating one of my favorite movies. The sign inside my back door reminds me every day, "There is always, always, always something to be thankful for."

Is It Over Yet?

AN INTERVIEWER ASKED ME RECENTLY, "Which was more difficult—going to college or going to work?" First of all, this is a very good question and one that I had never been asked before. Thinking about my answer, I quickly took into account how often I held my breath with each of those situations and pressed forward through my fears. Like watching a scary movie when I was a kid, there were times when it felt like all I could do was close my eyes tight, take a deep breath, and wonder to myself, *is it over yet?*

"Are you sure this is what you want to do, Allison?"

"Yes, I'm sure."

"Because I'm not even sure this is going to work out the way we hope it will. You need to be absolutely certain you're ready for this." The rehabilitation counselor assigned to me by the state was just being cautious. After all, it was his job to justify allocating funds to help me begin college at Auburn University at Montgomery. Ultimately, my parents would end up covering my tuition and living expenses, while a scholarship and Alabama's Rehabilitation Services would pay for books and my attendant's salary. If I wasn't serious about this decision, it would never work. By the time I met my rehab counselor, however, I had been questioned by others and interrogated by myself so many times that I had no doubt in my mind what I wanted.

I was going to college. I was moving away from home just as my sister had done. Until one month before I was scheduled to begin classes, I still didn't know who was going to care for me at school. The young girl we hired to be my first live-in attendant was an eighteen-year-old freshman just like me. We had found her by word of mouth through a family member just in the nick of time for me to register for classes and reserve a room in the campus apartments. She was painfully shy, and she looked as frightened as I felt. My life would be in her hands. I had no idea how capable those hands might be or how long she would be willing to stay with me. I had no idea how or if I'd be able to replace her if she did leave. I had no idea how or if I could physically handle the workload of college classes. On the day my parents drove me to Montgomery in August of 1989, the only two things I knew for sure were that I was going to college and that I was moving away from home just as my sister had done.

Going to work was also frightening, but in a different way.

"I hope you don't mind my asking, but what special accommodations will you need?"

"Probably none, as long as I have a desk or table that I can reach."

"Okay. Well, I have to say you took me by surprise, but you've been highly impressive. If you could get through graduate school, I shouldn't doubt your ability to do this job." The surprise my future boss was referring to was that I had not told him about my disability when I called requesting a job interview.

Upon college graduation, finding employment was totally up to me. My goal had been to move to Nashville, Tennessee, but after months of trying to force my strategy to work out, I trusted that it was not in

God's plan, and I moved my life in a different direction. The opening for a master's level mental health therapist in Russellville, Alabama, seemed to be the perfect fit for me. I met all of its qualifications, and the job required no traveling, which meant that I could go to work without my attendant. Not disclosing my disability when I initially inquired about the job was not meant to be deceptive. It was simply an expression of who I had become. I was no longer defined by my disability.

During college, I had succeeded on a level I had previously thought impossible. I had found and hired live-in attendants through local newspapers, had kept up with notes and tests by writing with my mouth, and had remained on the dean's list for the first two years. I had lived an independent lifestyle for over six years. Graduating with a master's degree in counseling in May of 1996, I knew I had proven all there was to prove.

In the job interview, I likened my future employer's taking a chance on me to taking a shot in the dark—only the bravest soul would attempt it. I admitted that I did not always know how I would accomplish certain tasks, but I promised I would always find a way. One week later, the chance was bravely offered, and I accepted.

Facing the unknown still made me cringe. Whenever that old, familiar fear crept in, I'd find myself biting my lip and asking, "Is it over yet?" By then though, I had learned to keep breathing. Fear was always going to be a part of my life, simply because new mountains were around every corner, and no one else knew how to climb them either. I was learning to make peace with uncertainty. In preparation for the next step of my journey—going to work in September of 1996—I took a deep breath and understood that it was not over yet. This time, that was okay.

Paper Clips

EVERY MORNING WHEN I GET to work, I go through a set of rituals. I grab the cup off my desk and head to the water fountain to fill it. My lunch consists of either a can of Slim-Fast, which a co-worker puts in the refrigerator for me, or a granola bar, which I place on my desk. I then begin the task of turning on my computer.

When I first got my job, I did all of my paperwork by writing with my mouth. I kept up pretty well, given that a typical mental health chart can exceed the length of *War and Peace*. Eventually, I was given the option of using dictation, which I gladly accepted. However, when technology finally computerized our paperwork, I was thrilled. With my dowel stick, I can peck faster than most people can with their fingers, and I enjoy doing it. There was just one small problem with using my computer at work: starting it up. It is a physical impossibility to press the *control*, *alternate*, and *delete* buttons simultaneously with one dowel stick, so I did what I have always done. I found a way to make it work. Using two bent paper clips that I wedge in my keyboard, I hold down two of the buttons while I push the other. Sometimes this works on the first try,

57

but most of the time it does not. Nevertheless, this is how I begin every weekday morning.

When I first began my career, I knew I would have to go to work without an attendant. At the same time, I had no idea how I would manage things. For the first eighteen months, I was asked to share an office with a co-worker. I could not have received a better blessing at that time. Alan seemed to instinctively know the balance between helping and letting me do things on my own. He listened to my fears but confronted me when I allowed them to take over.

A perfect and humorous example of how I view myself and my disability happened one day while I conversed with Alan. We were discussing my future and how I might be able to continue my independent lifestyle as I grew older. Alan suggested I look into assisted living homes. In all seriousness, I replied, "Oh, Alan, I couldn't do that. Those are for people with serious disabilities." As long as I live, I will never forget the look on Alan's face. His expression seemed to say, "You really don't know, do you?" Trying hard to prevent laughing and hurting my feelings, he blurted out, "Allison, you have no limbs!" When Alan left to take another job, I was nervous, but I knew he was leaving me better prepared to face whatever came next.

As time went by, I learned through trial and error how to get things done at work. For instance, I discovered that stocking up on forms and having them placed within my reach would cut down on needing to ask for them so often. When I mastered the art of using the Xerox machine, my long time co-workers, Janice Nelson and Anita Coffman, were just as ecstatic as I was. My clients help distribute the handouts that are needed in my therapy groups. I've even learned how to use the shredder. These anecdotes illustrate the mundane tasks people do every day at work without a second thought but for me took years of practice.

Whenever frustration sets in at your own office, never forget what can be accomplished with time, determination, and two paper clips!

I'm Not Independent

THROUGHOUT THIS BOOK, THE WORD "independent" appears frequently, because independence has been a lifelong goal for me. It was all I dreamed of as a child, and it's what I've worked to attain my entire adult life. Now, after living up to my idea of independence, I am reevaluating its definition and importance in my life.

I have achieved the life I have always wanted; I work in the profession of my choice. Years ago, many people suggested I choose a field that incorporates my disability on some level, such as rehabilitation counseling or advocating for the disabled. Instead I chose to do what has always come naturally to me: I listen to other people's problems and do my best to help solve them. I have a house with a mortgage in my own name, which is oddly a source of satisfaction for me. I essentially come and go as I please. I enjoy shopping in home decor stores, eating out, and going to the movies. I'm forever looking forward to upcoming visits with family and friends. My pets, a chocolate Lab named Sadie and a cat named Natchez, mean the world to me. For all outward appearances, I live a "normal" life that is not limited by disability. I finally fit into the picture of independence that I had always imagined.

There is another side to this story, however. Every morning someone has to give me a shower, dress me, and brush my teeth. Someone has to drive me to and from work every day. Most of the time I do feed myself, but someone has to prepare the food I eat. Someone has to do my laundry and keep my house in order. I pay my own bills, but someone has to get the mail out of the box.

I estimate that I have had around twenty-five live-in attendants since my first year in college. Some stayed a week and some stayed over a year. Some left only to come back later. Some took advantage of my situation and stole from me, while others learned to better appreciate their own blessings. Over the years, I have come to refer to all of them as "my girls." My life experiences with them have been as varied as the individuals themselves. With each attendant, a whole new life intersects with mine. I liken the experience to marrying someone you have just met or getting a brand-new set of limbs every six months or so. The adjustment is always difficult at the beginning, but the lessons I learn are always worth it in the end. I would not make it without my girls.

There have been a few times when I have had difficulty finding live-in attendants. Thankfully, my mother stayed with me during those lapses. My skill in seeking and finding suitable attendants has improved greatly, however, and I have not been without one for several years.

In an effort to console a friend, I once made the statement, "It's okay to need support sometimes. Don't you need support?" I might as well have been saying this to myself. Accepting and making peace with my own dependence on others has been an uphill battle. The physical dependence was easier to swallow than my emotional need for others. In my mind, I could not justify both. It was only when I saw my total dependence on God that my walls came down. They were shattered by sheltering love that allowed me the freedom to breathe. I could trust again, because the Source of my being was trustworthy. In admitting my need, there was nothing to fear. There was only love and a gentle reminder of a universal truth, "Sure I need support. I'm not independent."

Photographs

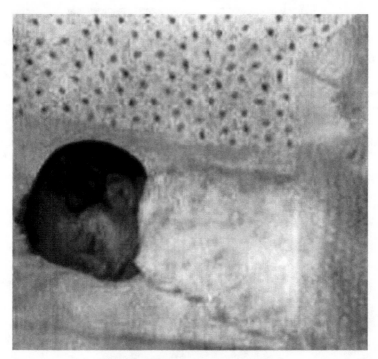

Allison Eighteen Days Old

Allison Nine Months

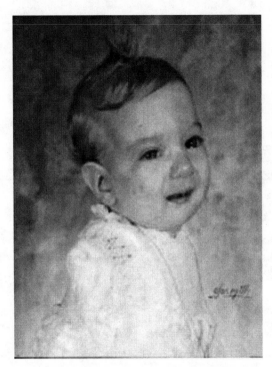

Allison Eighteen Months

Allison in Her First Walker

Allison Two Years Old

Allison and Dana 1974

Allison 1977

Allison and Father 1977

Parents Charlie and Gloria Wetherbee 1978

Allison and Megan 1978

Allison and Donette Dunagan-Mullinix at Camp ASCCA 1978

Megan, Allison, and Dana 1981

Allison High School Graduation 1989

Allison and Natchez 1995

Allison 2006

Allison and mother 2007

Dana, Allison, and Megan 2007

Parents Charlie and Gloria Wetherbee 2005

Part Two:

Devotions and Inspirations

All or Nothing

John 9:1–3

As Jesus was walking along, he saw a man who had been blind from birth. "Rabbi," his disciples asked him, "Why was this man born blind? Was it because of his own sins or his parents' sins?" "It was not because of his sins or his parents' sins," Jesus answered. "This happened so the power of God could be seen in him."

Psalm 71:7

My life is an example to many, because you have been my strength and protection.

My life is full of extremes. I have always lived with an all-or-nothing mentality. In my world, it's sink or swim. I adopted this attitude out of necessity. I don't feel as if I had much choice in the matter. I was born into a life that demands my full effort. When I do not give my all to something, I am not successful with it. There are no easy outs or short cuts for me. In all the jobs I've had, I have never known prior to starting exactly how I would be able to do the required tasks. My answer to this problem has been a simple one: I jump without a parachute and learn how to fly.

As a child, one of the first lessons I had to accept was that no one would be able to teach me how to do certain things. There were no instructions or blueprints to follow. To a large extent, I have had to teach myself how to maneuver in this life. For example, no one else could show me how to hold and angle a pencil in my mouth. It took years of practice to achieve the writing skills that match most other people's. No one could show me how to open a door using my chin or how to pick up a phone receiver using my mouth. I learned on my own how to manipulate makeup brushes with my shoulders to apply cosmetics. I learned how to type on a keyboard using a dowel stick. Through the grace of God, I have learned how to maintain an independent lifestyle despite my disability.

I often hear the comment, "I would never be able to do what you do." The fact is, though, we can all do whatever is asked of us. Whatever lot in life that we have been given, God also gives us a way to use it for His glory. For every problem, He does provide a solution. We just have to be willing to see it and do it. We are to use what we have been given rather than dwell on what we do not have. God blessed me with a relentless spirit that does not know how to give up. Everyone has access to this same way of being. God provides the strength that is required to take on any challenge. It is then our responsibility to decide that quitting is not an option.

Let's Begin

Romans 13:9–10

For the commandments say, "You must not commit adultery. You must not murder. You must not steal. You must not covet." These—and other such commandments—are summed up in this one commandment: "Love your neighbor as yourself." Love does no wrong to others, so love fulfills the requirements of God's law.

2 Thessalonians 3:5

May the Lord lead your hearts into a full understanding and expression of the love of God and the patient endurance that comes from Christ.

Proverbs 2:7

He grants a treasure of common sense to the honest. He is a shield to those who walk with integrity.

In 2004, God decided to do some spring cleaning in my life. I had let tons of dust accumulate in the corners, and the remains of my poor choices filled my closets. An upheaval was required.

Things had to change, so God got busy with me, and I became serious about Him. I was thirty-three years old. It was past time for me to get a grip and understand that just believing was not the same as letting Him lead. I had to surrender control and learn to depend on God.

He attracted my attention a few years earlier by allowing a set of circumstances, which I had started, to spin completely out of control. It was a situation where I knew better but I did it anyway. In my younger years, I had always felt God's presence guiding me out of my mistakes. This time however, it was as though He said, "Okay, if this is where you want to go, I won't stop you." So, I had leapt head first into a pile of chaos that was so thick I thought I'd never see daylight again, but eventually the fog did lift, and the sun did rise. That's when God spoke again and told me, "Now, let's begin."

I must admit, I had many misconceptions of what a life led by God would look like. First of all, I had to get rid of the stereotypes in my mind. I, like many others, had an image of the "good Christian" stuck somewhere between my ears! That image painted the picture of someone who kept a permanent fake smile on her face to cover up the unbearable boredom of her life. It was also an image of someone who never had any fun. I realize this was a terribly unfair assessment, but it was my honest interpretation at the time. Honesty, by the way, is the key that unlocks this myth.

A life led by God means following the laws of honesty and love. Live an honest and loving life, and the rest of God's law will naturally follow. God created us and He doesn't want us to be anything other than what we are: His flawed children who need Him. He wants us to be real and genuine. He wants us to love Him with all our hearts and love others as ourselves.

Let me assure anyone who still has doubts, a life led by God is anything but dull. It is rich with creativity and learning. The longer you walk with Him, the more you know for sure that the possibilities are endless. The enthusiasm of childhood returns, and you can get excited about the future again. You can also afford to relax because it's not all about you anymore. Worrying becomes a waste of time rather than the hobby it used to be.

You also begin to listen to the inner voice of the Holy Spirit. It takes you in directions you never would have dreamed of going on your own. It reminds you to pray during thick and thin. It calls you to study God's word. It urges you to satisfy the longing to be baptized. It guides you to send Christmas cards to old friends and call new ones. It leads you to write your thoughts down, share them with people, and turn them into a book. Courage becomes abundant, because the Holy Spirit shows you that there is nothing to fear. God gives everyone their own unique path to the divine, and this has been mine.

There is no boredom in real honesty and unashamed love. You can speak with boldness like never before. You can tell people what you think and feel with a confidence that comes only from God. When you allow God to take over, the drama of life doesn't end. It just becomes deeper and more meaningful. The cheaper dramas, such as unhealthy relationships, worry over what others think of you, and the endless array of he said/she said scenarios, just don't hold the interest they once did. Instead, you realize that God offers something much more fulfilling. He has work for you to do. So, why waste time when you can begin now?

We're on the Same Side

Proverbs 1 3:10

Pride leads to conflict; those who take advice are wise.

Proverbs 17:19

Anyone who loves to quarrel loves sin; anyone who trusts in high walls invites disaster.

Proverbs 10:12

Hatred stirs up quarrels, but love makes up for all offenses.

Matthew 5:9

God blesses those who work for peace, for they will be called the children of God.

No one enjoys being criticized, and although we all know people who seem to feed off conflict, most of us don't care for it at all. For the most part, we are all just doing the best we can with what we have. We all try to be good parents, children, spouses, brothers, sisters, or friends. When we love someone, we do our best to be kind, considerate, and honest, but life is messy and we were made to make mistakes. Sometimes our most well-meaning actions are misunderstood. After we have given the people in our lives the best we have, the last thing we want is for them to find fault with us.

When this happens in my own life, my first reaction is hurt. No matter how my actions play out, I never intend to cause harm, so I tend to feel blindsided when my unwitting mistakes are called into question. More often than not, however, my hurt feelings are the result of comparing the person in front of me to someone who hurt me in the past. If the present situation reminds me of old criticisms, ancient wounds reopen. I become speechless with the fear that the past is suddenly repeating itself.

After the initial hurt has run its course, the anger sets in. Arguments pleading my case run through my head, and within a few short minutes, I'm convinced that I was right all along. Placing all the blame on the other person, I plan my rebuttal for when the subject reappears. I decide that my actions were perfectly logical and look forward to the next available opportunity to get the other person to see it my way as well!

I know that I am not alone in my reaction to conflict. My emotions and the conclusions I make based on those emotions are fairly typical. However, just because I find myself in good company does not mean that I am right. It is wrong of me to compare those who love me now to those who hurt me in the past. It is also wrong to refuel an argument with words of anger. After making many mistakes in the past, I am now finding a better way, one built on genuine love.

When I love someone, I am on his side, and hopefully he is on mine. We are on the same team working toward the same goals of happiness and well-being. Teammates look out for each other, take care of each other, and defend each other. When disagreements arise, they need to be dealt with openly and honestly. I don't want those I love to fear telling me the truth. I also don't want them to be afraid of my honesty. If something needs to be done or some behavior needs to be changed, all we should have to do is ask. The best resolver of conflict and healer of criticism that I have found begins and ends with respect. Where respect is present, there is not much room left for judgment or anger.

The people in our lives will fall short at times, because no one can stand on a pedestal of perfection. We are all flawed human beings just trying to live happily ever after. I used to believe that the greatest three words in the English language were "I love you," but experience has taught me different. It takes more than love for any relationship to survive the doubt that conflict causes. What will always keep us together is the promise of commitment. The five words that can make us walk through fire for each other are, "I will never leave you." No matter what happens, and no matter what we face, I will never leave you.

Home

Proverbs 27:8

A person who strays from home is like a bird that strays from its nest.

Ephesians 3:16-18

I pray that from his glorious, unlimited resources he will empower you with inner strength through his Spirit. Then Christ will make his home in your hearts as you trust in him. Your roots will grow down into God's love and keep you strong. And may you have the power to understand, as all God's people should, how wide, how long, how high, and how deep his love is.

Most people agree with the old saying, "You can't go home again." Countless songs and poems have been written about the common desire to relive life's simpler times. This quest seems eternal, and we can all relate to it. Can we really go home again?

Home is all that is familiar and sweet. Home is where we are loved, accepted, and appreciated for the unique beauty we offer to this world. Home is comfort and warmth. It is a true glimpse of heaven on earth. Home is not always a place on a map or any earthly location. It cannot always be found in a building, a house, or a backyard. We search for home in those places as we grow older, only to be disappointed when it is not there. Home cannot be contained in that way.

We search, sometimes for years, for what we hope will satisfy our yearning to belong. Usually, when we least expect it, God comes down. He guides a friend to lay his hand on our shoulder. He leads a loved one to rest her forehead against ours. He drives someone to spontaneously say "I love you" in the middle of a belly laugh. He compels old friends to reconnect while the time and space that have been between them go unnoticed.

Home is anything that offers beauty and tender affection. It is where we are loved, and it is where we belong. Home is where God is. We are welcomed there, and we can go there anytime we want.

Disabilities 101

Romans 1 2:10

Love each other with genuine affection, and take delight in honoring each other.

Philippians 2:3

Don't be selfish; don't try to impress others. Be humble, thinking of others as better than yourselves.

Sometimes it amazes me how much times have changed regarding people with disabilities.

For instance, there is a huge emphasis these days on appropriate terminology. In 1970, I was born with no arms or legs. Back then, I usually heard people refer to me with phrases like "crippled child" or "the little handicapped girl." Today, when people call my work looking for me but can't recall my name, they will ask for "the girl in the wheelchair." In our current politically correct world, I'm not sure which part of that latter phrase should offend me. Should it be the part that mentions the wheelchair? I have other distinguishing features the caller could point out, I guess. Or, should I be offended by the fact that I'm a woman who's being called a "girl"?

There is also the issue of how to interact with people with disabilities in public. This has also evolved a great deal throughout my lifetime. I can remember seeing mothers reprimanding their children for staring at me too much back when I was young. Many times, if a kid even so much as looked in my direction, their mom or dad would yank them up in no time flat. These days, some children are actually encouraged by their parents to walk right up and ask questions.

Recently, a child who appeared to be around eight years old approached me in Wal-Mart to boldly inquire, "How do you brush your teeth?" I must have looked surprised. Before I had a chance to respond, his mother stepped forward to inform me that she tells her children to ask questions whenever they need to find an answer. I guess this kid really needed to discover my method of tooth brushing right when I was trying to decide what flavor ice cream I wanted. I politely let the child know that someone brushes my teeth for me, and I thought to myself how much things really have changed over the years in very interesting ways.

The fact that more people with severe disabilities, like mine, are gaining more independence every day is something we should celebrate. Any time a group of people who were once held back or hidden by society altogether simply due to their differences finds a way to improve their lives, everyone benefits. It still seems to me, though, that when it comes to the appropriateness of people's reactions, things would naturally fall into place if everyone would simply maintain a logical balance. Children, and adults for that matter, will always look at those who are different and will want to ask questions. It is a natural thing to do, but simply using good manners truly goes a long way. When someone's curiosity burns, I find it very respectful if they begin with, "May I ask you a question?" That way, at least I have an idea what's coming. A little common sense is all that is required.

Having a disability sometimes causes awkward moments. For example, every time I meet someone new, there is always a moment of hesitation while the person desperately searches my body for a hand to shake. Priceless facial expressions are evoked at the moment of realization that I don't have hands. I have a friend who thoroughly enjoys turning this instant of natural embarrassment on its head. He jokingly introduces me by saying, "This is my friend Allison. Shake her hand."

Some people may see this as a cheap shot. I do not. No one gets hurt when a reality is exposed, even if that reality causes some discomfort. It is only the truth is ignored or hidden that people get hurt. Dealing with a disability is already difficult enough. Taking it too seriously just makes it even harder than it has to be.

What, then, is the correct terminology? As far as I'm concerned, words are just words. We are the ones who associate either a negative or positive meaning. I have a co-worker who will not allow me to call myself "disabled" in front of him. To use Johnny Taylor's words, "I haven't yet found one thing that you are not able to do." I asked him one day, "Okay, what do you want me to call myself?" Without missing a beat, he answered, "Allison." That works for me.

The Hill Of Life

Proverbs 18:24

There are "friends" who destroy each other, but a real friend sticks closer than a brother.

John 15:13

There is no greater love than to lay down one's life for one's friends.

Ecclesiastes 4:9–12

Two people are better off than one, for they can help each other succeed. If one person falls, the other can reach out and help. But someone who falls alone is in real trouble. Likewise, two people lying close together can keep each other warm. But how can one be warm alone? A person standing alone can be attacked and defeated, but two can stand back-to-back and conquer. Three are even better, for a triple-braided cord is not easily broken.

Recently I heard about a conversation between a father and his daughter. They were talking about her new boyfriend. The father asked if the boyfriend would be able to climb the hill. His daughter asked, "What hill?" Her dad replied, "The hill of life. He's got to be able to climb it, because it's uphill all the way." When we look back on our lives, we can see that the father's statement is true. There are times when we struggle more than others. There are times when we reach a peak and can catch our breath, but we are all climbing in the same uphill direction.

Mountain climbers use a method called "belaying" to reach their destination. While one climber ascends, the other uses a rope to secure his safety. If the climber slips, his partner tightens the rope to avoid a fall. It is the partner's job to see that the climber arrives at the next step of the journey unharmed.

Recently a friend protested the disloyalty of a mutual acquaintance. In response I said, "I've been disloyal in the past. Why do you not ever question me about the things I've done wrong?" My friend answered, "You and I are different. You don't have to explain anything to me. You just stay with me and we'll be fine." With that one statement, I learned the definition of real friendship.

Fellow climbers who help me ascend the hill of life recognize their importance. They realize that most of the time their presence is all that's required. Just knowing they are there provides all the comfort I need to keep going. They know that they count on me in return. I have their backs, and they have mine. I have been blessed with friends who stay no matter what. These are the friends who teach what I want to learn. They stay involved with the daily happenings in my life without interfering or judging. They stay close through phone calls and visits but leave behind expectations and requirements. They stay accepting without criticizing or patronizing. They stay loving without manipulating and patient without controlling.

Friendship is a choice, and that is the beauty of it. We choose our friends and we choose our level of commitment to them. I am honored to have friends who have chosen to stay with me, and it is my privilege to stay with them. Whatever challenges the hill of life presents, it is nothing to fret over when you have brave friends holding the rope.

Say When

Proverbs 15:15–16

For the despondent, every day brings trouble; for the happy heart, life is a continual feast. Better to have little, with fear for the Lord, than to have great treasure and inner turmoil.

Matthew 11:29

Take my yoke upon you. Let me teach you, because I am humble and gentle at heart, and you will find rest for your souls.

We've all heard the offer, "I'll pour. Just say when." But if neither of you is paying attention, your mug will get filled to the brim and run over. Then you're forced to drop everything you were doing to clean up the sticky mess which would have been prevented had you not been so distracted in the first place. The kind gesture goes unnoticed as cross words fly, and yet another daily frustration is added onto an already over filled plate. There are times when life itself can feel this way.

In our modern society, sometimes I think we have gone too far over the edge. Advances in technology have spun our world into overdrive, and people are challenged just to keep up the pace. Working harder and faster to achieve greater productivity has become the norm. The bottom line is the only thing of importance in corporate America. People stretch themselves to the limit trying to maintain someone else's bottom line while lining the pockets of the powers that be. It seems that obtaining the American dream now requires living to work rather than working to live.

Making a living like this is bound to spill over into our personal lives. When we keep such a chaotic schedule, trying to preserve close family bonds is nearly impossible. The time is simply not there to give, but it is time together that strengthens relationships. It seems to me that time is our most valuable asset. It is priceless, because without it, love has no chance to grow.

Some people act as if love can be bought. Celebrities surround themselves with doting admirers whose care is motivated by cash flow. The pretense can continue for years while the person in the spotlight desperately tries to believe in the sincerity of hangers-on. When the financial well runs dry, however, the star is left alone with the realization of time wasted on disloyal souls. They may have fooled themselves into believing that love has a price, but they know better about time. Once time is lost, we cannot even dupe ourselves into believing we can buy it back. One of the hardest lessons in the world to learn is that once time has passed, it is gone forever.

When we give someone our time, we are honestly giving them the most precious gift we have to offer. Friendships mature with time, love deepens with time, and trust solidifies with time. Even children know that the measure of love they feel from others is equal to the amount of time they receive. When the majority of our time is spent running on life's treadmill, what is most important to us will surely suffer. Day after day, time slips by and love becomes distant.

Exhaustion and stress give way to bitterness that boils over into every aspect of our lives. In today's world, surviving in a permanent state of burnout seems to be a way of life, but it is no way to live.

Personally, I do not believe this is the way God intended for us to live. The words "joy," "love," and "peace" are repeated so often in the Bible that we must conclude God wants us to experience them. Superhuman professional achievement was never a part of God's plan for us. He doesn't ask us to try to be all things to all people, and He does not expect perfection. God encourages the simple life, and He taught us His greatest commandments through Jesus: to love Him with all we have and to love others as ourselves. He made it simple; we make it complicated.

The world will not stop spinning if we decide to slow things down. Life will go on even if we admit that we need a break. The mania that rules today's society will continue even as we accept that we need loving support and encouragement to keep going. None of us can lay down our obligations or responsibilities, but we all need help keeping the pressure of our lives from boiling over and making a mess of things. And we all have the right to say "when" if it ever becomes too much.

What If?

Matthew 10:29–31

What is the price of two sparrows—one copper coin? But not a single sparrow can fall to the ground without your Father knowing it. And the very hairs on your head are all numbered. So don't be afraid; you are more valuable to God than a whole flock of sparrows.

Isaiah 46:3–4

Listen to me, descendants of Jacob, all you who remain in Israel. I have cared for you since you were born. Yes, I carried you before you were born. I will be your God throughout your lifetime—until your hair is white with age. I made you, and I will care for you. I will carry you along and save you.

What would I do if I had arms? I ask myself this question every time I see the advances being made with prosthetic limbs. Science has not yet made me a candidate for artificial arms, but I can easily see it happening in the years to come. That hope naturally leads me to thoughts of how my life would be different. How much of my personality is defined by my disability? Would having limbs change me? Would I even want that change now that I have learned to adapt so well in the body God gave me?

Our experiences obviously play a huge role in whom we are and who we will become. We are not the same people we once were after living through major events like divorce or the death of a loved one. Changes alter the way we think and feel about ourselves, and they modify the way we relate to other people too. However, I believe that the core of who we are, our spirit, lives for eternity, remaining intact. It is this spirit that defines us.

Our souls have no beginning and no end. In the Bible, God assures us that we were known to Him before we were born. Our behaviors and habits may change as our time in this world takes its toll, but the spirit remains timeless and unbroken. Therefore, no person or circumstance can get the best of us unless we let them.

Having no arms or legs does not define who I am unless I allow it. When making decisions, I look at what I want and what feels right to me rather than what would be most "suitable" for a disabled person. More often than not, my choice leads me down the more difficult path, but staying true to myself is much more important to me than taking the easy way out. A long time ago, I decided that I would not shape my life around my disability.

If, by some miracle, someone invented arms that would work as real ones do, I would jump at the chance to use them. It wouldn't change me at all, but more of my personality would be shown, I believe. I would never buy a van again! Using hand controls, I would drive a truck or a jeep. I would give lots of hugs and hold lots of hands. At this stage in my life, dreams like these are no longer painful. They are simply reminders of what would be nice to have rather than longings for things needed. God provides for our needs, but He doesn't mind if we dream either. By the way, if they ever invent artificial legs that I could use, I'm buying a Harley!

I'm Sorry

Proverbs 17:9

Love prospers when a fault is forgiven, but dwelling on it separates close friends.

Luke 17:3–4

"If another believer sins, rebuke that person; then if there is repentance, forgive. Even if that person wrongs you seven times a day and each time turns again and asks forgiveness, you must forgive."

Last night I tossed and turned for hours churning a recent wrong into butter. This is fairly common for me. Whenever I have regret, it eats me alive. I cannot stand the thought of hurting or disappointing anyone. After replaying the occurrence in my mind a dozen times, I ask myself questions like, "How could I have done that? What was I thinking?" When I am honest with myself, the answer to these questions is always the same.

Anytime I take my eyes off the needs of others and instead choose selfishness, I regret it. To my eyes, selfishness is the source of all wrong. Human nature urges us to look out for number one, while our hearts remind us of our common interests. This tug of war between self and others is as old as time itself. Anytime that battle is lost, we all lose.

The misdeed that kept me awake last night would have never happened had I kept my attention on those around me. Their comfort needed to come before mine. Instead, I sought consolation for myself first. Nothing good followed that decision, and there was nothing I could do to take it back.

Later, when I realized the damage I had done, something amazing happened. After I expressed how sorry I was, I found that I had been forgiven even before the apology came. A miracle is defined in the dictionary as an event that appears inexplicable by the laws of nature and so is held to be an act of God. It feels like nothing short of a miracle when someone forgives you the exact moment you slip up.

Jesus makes it clear that repentance must come before forgiveness. If there is no remorse, then obviously no lesson was learned. At that point, trust is broken and the relationship is damaged. Thankfully, those who are closest to me know what is in my heart. They know that even when I do wrong, there is no ill intent and that an apology will soon follow.

I am still learning what real forgiveness is. It is a true gift that is given, not earned. It is given when love and devotion outweigh judgment and condemnation. Real forgiveness does not bring about pride or a free ticket to act any way we choose. Instead, it teaches us the true meaning of what it is to be humble. When I have wronged someone, I am not automatically entitled to forgiveness. When I am forgiven, I am grateful and saved. After accepting this gift, I fell sound asleep.

Misunderstandings

Proverbs 2:2–3

Tune your ears to wisdom, and concentrate on understanding.
Cry out for insight, and ask for understanding.

Philippians 1:9–10

I pray that your love will overflow more and more, and that you will
keep on growing in knowledge and understanding. For I want you
to understand what really matters, so that you may live pure and
blameless lives until the day of Christ's return.

There are two questions that I am asked often: "What is the most bizarre thing anyone has ever said to you?" and "What are the biggest misconceptions or misunderstandings about your disability?"

My answer to the first question has stood the test of time. It's an occasion that has been ingrained in my memory since I was eleven years old. I had just been named the Alabama Easter Seals Child of 1982 and had been asked to do several interviews for local and statewide newspapers and television programs. I was scheduled to appear on a noontime talk show at a local news station. A married couple from my hometown who volunteered for Easter Seals drove me to the interview. I was so nervous during the entire trip that I barely spoke a word. I had already seen myself on television a few times, but I had not done a live broadcast yet, and I was old enough to understand that if anything went wrong, there was nothing that could be done about it. I was actually sweating by the time we got to the station!

Several minutes before I was scheduled to go on the air, the interviewer came to prep me for what to expect. She said she would ask simple questions, like where I was from. Then she started asking specifically about my disability. I will never forget her words. She started out, "Now, you were born like this, right?" I nodded yes.

"And you have no limbs, right?" Again, I nodded yes.

"And it's a permanent condition?" I must have given her a puzzled look, because she decided to clarify her question.

"What I mean is, well, will you ever have arms or legs?"

Now, if I had been just a little older with just a little more experience behind me, I would have taken that question and run with it. I would have looked her straight in the face without cracking a smile and said something like, "Yes, I'm expecting them to grow any minute now." Unfortunately, I wasn't older. I was eleven, and instead of jolting her back to reality with a great comeback, I started crying. The friends who were with me calmed me down, assured me that she would not ask that question on the air, and got me ready to proceed with the interview. Thankfully, all went well.

My answer to the second question came to life not too many years ago. It involves an attitude that I have sensed on many occasions from many different people. The incident that follows depicts the only time this attitude has been expressed aloud in my presence. It happened one night while I was getting ready for bed.

The girl who was taking care of me at the time was brushing my hair. All of a sudden, she said, "You are so lucky." Unsure, I asked what she meant. She went on, "Well, it must be nice to just be able to sit all day and have other people do everything for you. You don't have to deal with anything. Everything's given to you and done for you. You don't even have to brush your own hair. I would love that!"

After talking with her about her comment, I knew she wasn't being mean and she wasn't joking. She was serious. Sadly, there are people who take their God-given abilities and blessings for granted so much that they are actually jealous of me. A friend once told me that my mere presence seems to make some people feel uncomfortable because it draws attention to their own insecurities. There are also people who resent having to help me with things that I am not able to do on my own. I'm thankful that these attitudes are the exception rather than the rule because I find them very difficult to understand. The fact is I would do anything to be able to brush my own hair and not have to ask for any help with simple, everyday chores. But this is my life, and I have made peace with it.

People tell me all the time that I make my life and my disability look easy. Fortunately, God did bless me with an attitude and a personality that accentuate what I can do rather than what I cannot. However, that does not mean that it is easy. This is something that the people who are closest to me understand very well. Whether I like to admit it or not, they understand that everything I do takes triple the effort. They recognize that it is not easy for me, but that I choose to do it anyway. They appreciate every opportunity to support me in any way possible, and they can't imagine how much I appreciate them in return.

So many people these days seem to expect to be given something for nothing. Sadly, there is a portion of our society that spends large amounts of time searching for schemes to avoid having to actually earn anything. My dream as a child was to have a home of my own, to have a job, and to live as independently as possible. My dreams have come true. I agree with anyone who says that I am lucky, but contrary to some people's beliefs, what I have has not been given to me. My good fortune is due to the kind of luck that is God given. God created a process by which anyone can achieve this kind of luck. This process is better known as work.

Who Do We Think We Are?

Romans 12:7–8

If your gift is serving others, serve them well. If you are a teacher, teach well. If your gift is to encourage others, be encouraging. If it is giving, give generously. If God has given you leadership ability, take the responsibility seriously. And if you have a gift for showing kindness to others, do it gladly.

Matthew 23:11–12

The greatest among you must be a servant. But those who exalt themselves will be humbled, and those who humble themselves will be exalted.

How important are we? How much do our little lives really matter in the grand scheme of things? If we are really honest about it, we act as if everything revolves around us at times. If you don't believe that, think about how bent out of shape we get when things don't go our way or unfold as we had planned. How do we act when the car won't start or when the bank mistakenly fails to show a deposit? At that moment, how many of us remind ourselves of the countless people who don't own a car or have never had a bank account in their name? Unfortunately, most of us would have to admit a level of selfishness that should make us feel ashamed.

Then again, the opposite side of the coin is also true. Far too often, we act as if we are weak and insignificant. Think about how it feels to see starving children on TV. Do we immediately pick up the phone and dial the number, believing that our thirty cents a day can save a child from starvation? Or do we tell ourselves that in the face of seemingly insurmountable problems, it would do no good for us to stand tall and be counted? Anytime we turn away from others in pain, no matter what form that pain takes, we sell ourselves short. We act as if the voice of love that God gave us doesn't have the power to change things.

The fact is that the moon will keep rising at the end of the day to brighten the night sky whether we are here to enjoy it or not. The birds will keep singing to greet the world every morning. The earth will continue to revolve around the sun when we are no longer here for it to revolve around! Things will move along just fine as God sees fit, with us or without us. While we are here, however, we do have the power to touch people's lives. We have a choice and a responsibility to use that power wisely and with loving intent. We were put here on this earth for one reason: to love and to care for each other. That is our divine purpose. We never know how important our actions may be to another person. We need to remember that the results of our actions can be endless as well as timeless.

So, just how important are we? As unique creations of God, we are inconceivably important. As the Lord's humble servants, we bow down in the knowledge that none of it is about us. When we set our hearts on the fact that everything we do is covered by His grace, how important we are no longer matters.

Funny Things

Ecclesiastes 3:1 & 4

For everything there is a season, a time for every activity under heaven.
A time to cry and a time to laugh. A time to grieve and a time to dance.

Luke 6:21

God blesses you who are hungry now, for you will be satisfied.
God blesses you who weep now, for in due time you will laugh.

Proverbs 31:25–26

She is clothed with strength and dignity, and she laughs without fear of the future. When she speaks, her words are wise, and she gives instructions with kindness.

Proverbs 17:22

A cheerful heart is good medicine, but a broken spirit saps a person's strength.

A strange phenomenon has happened in my life many times over. Thankfully, I have always seen the humor in it, even as a child. I witnessed this oddity for the first time while sitting at a busy lunch table at camp. The dining hall was very loud as people busily fixed their plates. From the other end of the table, I heard someone ask, "Will you please pass the ketchup?"

I, of course, continued looking around never once considering the possibility that they were speaking to me. That is until I heard a frustrated voice say, "Allison, hand me the ketchup, please." I was totally bewildered. This had never happened before, so I had absolutely no idea what to do. A person who had eaten meals with me every day for weeks had forgotten my disability. In all politeness, I responded, "I'm sorry, but I don't have any hands."

Thus, the strangest phenomenon of my life had begun. How on earth could anyone who has seen me, much less spent time with me, forget that I have no arms or legs? You would think something like that is fairly unforgettable, but I am nonetheless amused every time someone asks, "You know how it feels when your arm goes to sleep?" Another common one is, "Do you have any fingernail clippers?" Most of the time, I just continue the conversation and wait for the moment to come when they figure it out on their own. The longer it takes for them to remember, the greater the laugh is when they do. With scarlet cheeks, they usually say something like, "I'm sorry, I just didn't think about it. You seem so normal." I have always taken this as one of the best compliments I can receive. Even though I have never known how to define "normal," other people seem to think that I fit their definition of it very well.

I believe that people forget my differences simply because I do not act as though I'm different. I'm not a victim of my disability or of any other circumstance, for that matter. I've been given all I need, as we all have, to make peace with the hand I've been dealt. A life focused on abundance rather than lack naturally produces more abundance. Attitude is determined by choice, and it's a decision we make every day. If I ever stop finding the humor in my situation, it will be the end of me.

People often ask me, "What is the most difficult thing about your disability?" I used to think that feeling like a burden is my biggest difficulty, but recently I have come to see that this feeling is rooted in selfishness and that it's unrealistic. Valuable time is wasted on such self-absorbed matters, and God never intended for anyone to feel guilty for refusing to sit life out.

As for the reply I give to others regarding the greatest difficulty of my disability, I have never been able to provide a serious answer. The question just poses too tempting an opportunity to pass up. With a straight face and a somber expression, I usually say, "chiggers."

Bad Company

Proverbs 13:20

Walk with the wise and become wise; associate with fools and get in trouble.

Proverbs 14:7

Stay away from fools, for you won't find knowledge on their lips.

Proverbs 12:26

The godly give good advice to their friends; the wicked lead them astray.

2 Timothy 2:22

Run from anything that stimulates youthful lusts. Instead, pursue righteous living, faithfulness, love, and peace. Enjoy the companionship of those who call on the Lord with pure hearts.

My mother used to tell me to be very careful about the company I keep. I thought she just worried too much, and being the stubborn girl I was, I refused to heed her advice. However, after many wrong turns, I discovered the hard way that my mama was right. Fools do walk among us. We know this not just because we see them in our daily lives. We also know fools are in our midst because the Bible tells us so.

The Bible teaches difficult truths that are often overlooked. With our limited understanding, it is hard to reconcile tolerance and wisdom, but that is exactly what the Bible calls us to do. This struggle has plagued me for years. In my effort to be relentlessly forgiving, I have a long history of accepting unacceptable behavior. The result is predictable. While I worked to clean up someone else's pigsty, their slop got slung on me.

This is an inevitable reality. The old saying, "It's easier to pull others down than up," is absolutely true. Gravity is a powerful force that holds us to the earth. Trying to pull someone out of spiritual deprivation against their will is about like fighting gravity. More often than not, when exhaustion kicks in, the one with the tightest grip loses their footing and falls head first into the fire below. We pay a high price when we refuse to let go.

Keeping bad company can also lead to identity theft. We hear every day in the news of someone losing their identity at the hands of crooks. It's as if the victim's whole life is tarnished, and they are forced to start all over again. This can also happen spiritually. Our spiritual identity is based on our beliefs, values, and actions. When our lives are consumed with anyone who turns his face from God, our spiritual identity is in danger. It is a scientific fact that we are what we eat. If all we have to swallow is what a fool dishes out, our very substance is bound to be altered in an unhealthy ways.

The good news is that we always have a choice, and the even better news is that the Bible teaches how to choose. The fact that we are free to decide who will be our closest companions in this life is an awesome responsibility. Our spiritual integrity rides on it. Of course we are to help those living in darkness find the light, but we should not become involved to the point where we begin to live in darkness ourselves. The Bible clearly teaches that our closest relationships must be with trustworthy people who encourage our walk with God while we encourage theirs. As with many other matters in life, God makes it simple; we make it complicated.

Angels Are Watching

Hebrews 13:1–2

Keep on loving each other as brothers and sisters. Don't forget to show hospitality to strangers, for some who have done this have entertained angels without realizing it!

Hebrews 1:14

Therefore, angels are only servants—spirits sent to care for people who will inherit salvation.

Psalm 91:11–12

For he will order his angels to protect you wherever you go. They will hold you up with their hands so you won't even hurt your foot on a stone.

A co-worker once asked me if I believe in angels. Without blinking, I answered, "Absolutely!" My mother has always believed that a guardian angel is with me at all times. Each time I told her about a close call, such as almost falling out of my chair at school, her unfailing response was, "That's your guardian angel protecting you." As a child, I thought she said those words for comfort's sake. As an adult, I believe with all of my heart that there is a supernatural spirit watching over me. My guardian angel has never let me down.

I also believe that my guardian angel has gotten a new assistant in the last few years. My maternal grandfather passed away in 2000. His grandchildren affectionately called him, "Big Daddy." Big Daddy had earned his name as a large man who closely resembled John Wayne in his younger years. When I was a child, he delighted in holding me as a captive audience in his lap, entertaining me with his pocket watch and stories about hunting. As I grew older, I made a point of showing interest in Big Daddy's favorite hobby, gardening. Every time I visited my grandparents, I asked him to show me what he had planted and what was growing well. I am not sure which one of us got the most joy out of those last few visits to Big Daddy's garden. We both appreciated every minute that we had because we knew our time was limited.

A few months after Big Daddy died, I felt his presence with me so strongly one night that I could have sworn I saw him. Whether I actually saw his image or not, I know for a fact that he was making himself known to me. I felt completely assured that night that Big Daddy was still taking pleasure in watching me grow older, just as he always had.

There are many references to angels throughout the Bible. Angels are not fabricated by Hollywood to decorate motion pictures. They are actual holy beings. Every day we are also surrounded by earthly angels who come to us in the form of friends, family, or even strangers. God sends His comfort, strength, and love through people. Whenever your soul is touched with goodness, it is through the hand of God. Yes, I do believe in angels. Earthly and heavenly alike, they are created and led by the same loving God.

Never Stop Learning

1 Timothy 4:10–12

This is why we work hard and continue to struggle, for our hope is in the living God, who is the Savior of all people and particularly of all believers. Teach these things and insist that everyone learn them. Don't let anyone think less of you because you are young. Be an example to all believers in what you say, in the way you live, in your love, your faith, and your purity.

Romans 12:2

Don't copy the behavior and customs of this world, but let God transform you into a new person by changing the way you think. Then you will learn to know God's will for you, which is good and pleasing and perfect.

Wynonna Judd said in an interview a few years ago, "Teach what you want to learn." In other words, instead of sitting around waiting to learn something, go ahead and do it. If you want to learn how to have more love in your life, be more loving. If you want forgiveness or patience, be more forgiving and patient. The list is endless. Judd's quote has stayed with me all of these years, because it calls me to take responsibility for myself and to take action. It acknowledges that none of us have reached our highest level of awareness, and it challenges us to do something about it.

This reflects my chosen way of living. I may get down at times, but getting out is never an option. I'm in this life to push it as far as I can. I pray that my desire to keep leaning, growing, and improving as a person never leaves me. Sitting back acting as if I've reached my pinnacle simply because the big challenges have been overcome is simply not my style. Even bigger challenges are coming down the road, and if I don't prepare now, I won't be ready then. I want to learn from every test that life hands me so that I can be stronger and wiser when the next obstacle is thrown in my path.

There are people who face every crisis the same way each time. They seem to never learn that it can be done differently. It's as if they believe that life is supposed to be easy, and they fall apart when it's not. Life has never been easy. It's been difficult from the beginning of time, and I doubt that will change any time soon. Accepting this simple fact of life and moving past it diminishes the emotional turmoil caused by life's problems. Misfortune no longer holds the power to shock us. When we are willing to learn from life's difficulties, each new trouble seems less significant.

I want to teach what I want to learn. I want to grow stronger in the faith that things will work out in God's time according to God's will. I also want to relax in the knowledge that I'm surrounded by people who are heading in the same direction as I am. We are all each other's teachers and we are all each other's students. We don't give in. We don't give up. And we will reach our destination right on time.

Small Acts of Love

1 Corinthians 13:3–8:13

If I gave everything I have to the poor and even sacrificed my body, I could boast about it; but if I didn't love others, I would have gained nothing.

Love is patient and kind. Love is not jealous or boastful or proud or rude. It does not demand its own way. It is not irritable, and it keeps no record of being wronged. It does not rejoice about injustice but rejoices whenever the truth wins out. Love never gives up, never loses faith, is always hopeful, and endures through every circumstance.

Prophecy and speaking in unknown languages and special knowledge will become useless. But love will last forever!

Three things will last forever—faith, hope, and love—and the greatest of these is love.

"We can do no great things; only small things with great love." This quote by Mother Teresa is one of my favorites of all time. It is woven into a tapestry that has hung on the wall in my office for years. I like it, because it reminds me of what to strive for. I may not hit the mark every day, but I do give it my best shot. Luckily, God did not put any of us here to fix all of the world's problems. Individually, it is not our job to set all wrongs right or to heal all wounds. Only God can do that, and He uses us all collectively to slay the mightiest of dragons. He has given the soldiers in His army a means of attack against injustice. I believe that in fighting the darkness we see every day, we are to use the most powerful weapon God gave us: His love.

It may sound odd to view love as a weapon, but if you have ever faced the demons of anger, isolation, or hurt, you know that it can feel like a fight. And if the battle was won, it was probably won with the powerful weapon of love.

We tend to use the word "love" very loosely in our society. We say things like "I love ice cream." We describe our material enjoyment with comments like "I love my new car." Sadly, there are those who use the word "love" to manipulate or control. An abuser may utter the words "I love you" after a verbal or physical beating. The word "love" gets thrown around so much that it is extremely easy to forget its true meaning, but one thing about love is for sure: once you have experienced it, you never forget how it feels.

Real love is unmistakable and undeniable. It is strong. It is a force powerful enough to release pain that has been held for decades. It can give you the courage to stand up and fight against all evil. Love provides the endurance and encouragement to chase your dreams. It supplies the gentleness needed to hold you when you fall. There are a million different ways to describe love. The best way I know is that love is what's behind all that is good, right, and just in this world. Love does not hurt. The only time that love causes pain is when it is missed. Mother Teresa's quote does not mean that great things cannot be done. Great things are done every day when God's gift of love is used. The mountains in our lives can, and do move. They are moved with one small act of love at a time.

Dance with Me in Heaven

2 Corinthians 5:1–3

For we know that when this earthly tent we live in is taken down (that is, when we die and leave this earthly body), we will have a house in heaven, an eternal body made for us by God himself and not by human hands. We grow weary in our present bodies, and we long to put on our heavenly bodies like new clothing. For we will put on heavenly bodies; we will not be spirits without bodies.

John 14:1–7

"Don't let your hearts be troubled. Trust in God, and trust also in me. There is more than enough room in my Father's home. If this were not so, would I have told you that I am going to prepare a place for you? When everything is ready, I will come and get you, so that you will always be with me where I am. And you know the way to where I am going." "No, we don't know, Lord," Thomas said. "We have no idea where you are going, so how can we know the way?" Jesus told him, "I am the way, the truth, and the life. No one can come to the Father except through me. If you had really known me, you would know who my Father is. From now on, you do know him and have seen him!"

The promise of continued life is God's gift to us through the grace of forgiveness. Our gift to God is our worship, praise, obedience, and thanksgiving. We are eternally grateful because we have been forgiven through the sacrifice of Jesus. As believers in the Son of God, we will forever live in a paradise that exceeds all imagination. The Bible's blueprint of heaven provides brief glimpses of the New Jerusalem, illuminated by God's light. There we will see angels, mansions, and streets of gold.

We also have the certainty of receiving new, heavenly bodies made by the hand of God. Our renewed bodies, we are told, will not be just spirit. In our life to come, we will dwell for eternity in brand new bodily form. In heaven there will be no pain and no cause for sadness. The only tears shed will be tears of joy. There will be no more longing to be freed from the bondage we experience in our current conditions. There will be no disabilities or death. All calamities will be resolved. All hurt will be healed. All imperfections will be made perfect. We will be made new.

I revel in full faith that one day I will experience all of the simple pleasures that have eluded me here. I believe that in heaven I will finally know what it is like to wade barefoot through a clear stream. I will know how it feels to hold someone's hand in mine. For the first time, I will have the heavenly pleasure of wrapping my arms around my loved ones. The realization of these promises makes me want to dance! Shall we?

Epilogue

WHEN I FIRST WROTE THE story "I Was Born This Way," I didn't even consider turning it into a book. It was only when the subsequent stories began taking shape that I realized this book was forming itself. The stories flowed in chronological and emotional sequence. By the time I made the decision to write a book, I realized that I already had. At that point, all I really had to do was put the stories together and fill in the blanks.

The completion of this book is a perfect metaphor for my life in general. When I start something, I usually have no idea what I'm doing, but if I just keep going, the pieces eventually fall into place. There are no coincidences, as my life has shown. Things don't just happen. Instead, I believe that situations occur, even difficult ones, to take me to the next step of my journey and to mold me into the person I am meant to be. In the end, I am left with a completed puzzle put together by the hand of God.

As I write this epilogue, I am sitting in my new home at Easter Seals Camp ASCCA. On December 22, 2007, I relocated and began working here as the director of public relations.

Exactly two years earlier, I decided to send a Christmas card to my old friends that I had met through Camp ASCCA many years before, Sam and Glenda Hetherington. I had lost touch with all of my camp friends and had not even visited the camp itself in seventeen years, but by the end of 2006, with the help of the Camp ASCCA Web site, my life was full of new memories and reconnected friendships. At about the same time that I was sending out the first version of this book to family and friends in the summer of 2007, I was also offered my new job by the camp administrator John Stephenson.

As usual, at the beginning of this transition I had no idea what I was doing. In essence, I was leaving everything that I had worked for, including my home and my profession of eleven years, to enter a brand new life. I was scared, but I did my best to concentrate on the hope that this new life would work as well as the old one had. When my house in Russellville sold after only two months on the market, I heard angels sing! I wanted to see it as a sure sign that all would be well.

Since moving here, I have fallen in love with Camp ASCCA all over again. Although I love my job and my life at camp, being here has not gone as smoothly as I had hoped. Keeping and finding good personal care attendants has not been easy. At this very moment, I am in the search for my fourth roommate in less than a year. These adjustments have been difficult, but every day I find myself thanking God for allowing me to be here. Right now, all I know for sure is that I'm not giving up.

Tomorrow I plan to begin the process of self-publishing this book. I have no idea who will be my attendant at the time of its release. But as I told a friend recently, I made the decision a few years ago to not ever place my life on hold. Even in the midst of major obstacles, I can still choose to move forward.

Several years ago, I crafted refrigerator magnets that I have displayed ever since. On one of them, I wrote a quote by Dr. Maya Angelou which reads: "When someone tells you who they are, believe them." Sharing who I am is exactly what I have attempted to do in the pages of this book. In doing so, it has helped me accept myself as I am even more. It is my hope that these pages can also be used as a mirror to discover your own truth, and possibly, as a tool to help with any needed improvements! Through the experience of writing this book, the lesson I have learned is quite simple: surrender what needs to be surrendered and hold tight to what needs to be held tight. God will do the rest.

Thank you for reading this book. I hope you have enjoyed it and have found blessings in it. May God's peace be with you.

My love to you always,
Allison Wetherbee
September 2008

Printed in the United States
134415LV00003B/1/P